Eviva Maria

Madonna della Civita

Eviva Maria

Madonna della Civita

The eternal bond of the Itrani immigrants of Cranston, Rhode Island with their homeland of Itri, Italy, and their unwavering faith to the Madonna

Bernadette Conte

Copyright © 2014 by Bernadette Conte.

Library of Congress Control Number:		2014901457
ISBN:	Hardcover	978-1-4931-6750-0
	Softcover	978-1-4931-6749-4
	eBook	978-1-4931-6751-7

All rights reserved. No part of this book may be reproduced or transmitted in any form or by any means, electronic or mechanical, including photocopying, recording, or by any information storage and retrieval system, without permission in writing from the copyright owner.

This book was printed in the United States of America.

Rev. date: 06/20/2014

To order additional copies of this book, contact:
Xlibris LLC
1-888-795-4274
www.Xlibris.com
Orders@Xlibris.com
541362

Contents

Special Acknowledgments 9
Introduction 11

Chapter 1	Itri and Immigration to a New Land 19
Chapter 2	Maria Santissima della Civita... 26
Chapter 3	Visit to the Sanctuary... 38
Chapter 4	The Church 42
Chapter 5	The Miraculous Picture.. 44
Chapter 6	Rescue of the Madonna.. 50
Chapter 7	The Silver Statue 59
Chapter 8	Visit of Pope Giovanni Paolo II... 63
Chapter 9	The 225th Anniversary of the Crowning of the Madonna 66
Chapter 10	Discorso Don Michele Manzi 73
Chapter 11	Our Beginnings... 88
Chapter 12	Shepherd My People 97
Chapter 13	Societa Religiouse Pelligrinaggio Itrano 130
Chapter 14	Plans for the Maria SS della Civita Church 145
Chapter 15	A Pastor's Vision.. 162
Chapter 16	My Story... 172
Chapter 17	Home for the First Time 180
Chapter 18	Divine Intervention 184
Chapter 19	My Trip to Italy.. 197
Chapter 20	The Original Statue 215

To Maria Santissima della Civita, our spiritual mother who chose to be among our ancestors in Itri, Italy, and Knightsville, Rhode Island. She has blessed us for many generations. May she continue to lead and guide our children and offspring for all generations to come. *Totus Tuus.*

To my late husband, Raffaele "Ralph" C. Conte, who encouraged me to never give up when situations became difficult. I could not have accomplished any of this work without the support, love, and understanding of my husband and children, Katherine M. Conte and Ralph C. Conte Jr.

To my mother, Caterina "Gaetanina" Cardi Capotosto, who led and guided me in the right direction during my research and often gave me a command to write and remember. I am grateful to her for giving me documents and books regarding Maria Santissima della Civita. I would not have been able to share with the reader the inspired document of the "Discorso" had she not given it to me, for the greater glory of God.

SPECIAL ACKNOWLEDGMENTS

I wish to thank and acknowledge in a special way Paola Sepe, wife of my cousin Gianpaolo Cardi of Itri, who translated from Italian into English chapters in a book written by her award-winning author cousin, Pino Pecchia. Paola gave his book entitled *Tra Sacro e Pofano in Terra d'Itri* to me when I visited Itri in April 2013. I am grateful to Pino for allowing me to include various chapters from his writings in this book.

Pino (full name Giuseppe) Pecchia was born in Fondi in 1940, where he now resides. He is married and has three daughters. He worked at the Town Hall of Itri but has retired. He has a passion for his homeland history, and studies and collects information and evidences about Itri, where he lived for fifteen years. He also authored a book containing news about Itri in three languages, which is followed by the publication of the book *Tra Sacro e Profano in Terra d'Itri*, where he revisits places, traditions, and events in Itri from its beginnings to the present day (with translation in English by the native-speaker teacher Paola Sepe and the French teacher-professor Antonio Pecchia). The book was presented at one of the summer events in Itri, "Meet the Author," on August 23, 2003, at the auditorium of the Medieval Castle of Itri. He is the recipient of many literary awards. On December 27, 2008, he was appointed an Order of Merit of the Italian Republic. On March 25, 2009, the Town Hall of Itri conferred him the title of Honorary Citizen of the Town of Itri. (I authorize Ms. Bernadette Conte, domiciled in Cranston [Rhode Island], USA, the publication of my biographical notes with the following references: writer Pino [Giuseppe] Pecchia, Italy.)

Paola Sepe was born in 1958 and brought up in Salisbury, Zimbabwe (ex-Rhodesia). She is married and has two daughters. She attended the Dominican Convent High School in Salisbury. She then left Rhodesia and settled in Italy in 1977 and lives in Itri. Currently, she is a coteacher at the Italian High Schools and is a certified TESOL (teacher of English for students of other languages). Apart from translating minor works such as university students' theses or legal documents, she translated Mr. Pino Pecchia's work *Tra Sacro e Profano in Terra d'Itri* in the year 2003 and translated a second publication in the year 2012 written by Mr. Ruggiero di Lollo, an Italian artist who lives in Gaeta, Italy. The book is an illustrated autobiography of the author.

Reverend Robert Hayman, retired professor of history at Providence College and historian for the Diocese of Providence, Rhode Island, for the encouragement, counsel and documents he gave to me.

Robert M. Bucci, Jr. for translating Don Michele Manzi's document the "Discorso."

Introduction

I vividly remember the tremendous spiritual leadership I and many others experienced from Reverend Cesare Schettini, our dear pastor and founder of St. Mary's Church. Knightsville, a small town in Cranston, Rhode Island, was blessed with immigrants from Itri, Italy, who gave from their dire poverty to have their own Italian church. Father Schettini listened to the needs of his people whom he shepherded. He would often visit homes to encourage men and women not to become discouraged when times were difficult. He lovingly told children to report to religious instructions, which he himself taught. He answered questions in a gentle but firm manner. When a child asked, "*But who made God?*" he would reply, "*Remember that God always was and always will be. You must have faith. You must believe.*" He continued, "*God is love. You must love him with all your heart, with all your soul, with all your mind, and with all your strength. You must love your neighbor as yourself.*" His concerns were not about himself, for he lived frugally, but for the flock he was sent to shepherd.

Each week, long lines of children waited on the church steps to enter the church for their confessions to be heard. The frigid winter days were the most difficult. We walked to church, waited a long time in line, which seemed to be endless, for our turn to have our confessions heard. At times, one of us was told to go to the end of the line again, without explanation. Realizing that one of us had difficulty, Father Schettini wanted to know what happened, and most of the time, he tried to rectify the matter.

The elders loved him. He could be found often visiting his parishioner, eating their homemade goodies, and drinking homemade wine. He would always bring joy, laughter, and encouragement to his friends and parishioners.

Many could not read or write. My parents' home was one of the many homes for them to come to when letters arrived from Itri, Italy. They would interpret the letters for family and friends and would write return letters to their relatives who waited for a response. I can visualize the sobs and tears of those whose relatives sent them news of their families. During these visits, while drinking coffee and eating homemade sweets, the elders would discuss church, family, community problems, and events. Many of these events with the elders remained in my memory.

Their faith and love for Maria SS della Civita was unshakable. It got them through many hardships and sorrows. When time came to celebrate their feast, they did not spare anything. Children were included in the procession, whether or not they wanted to march. Girls marched in their first communion dresses, and the boys marched in the St. Anthony robes made by Madeline Pallotta, a member of the Knightsville community. We went to the long High Mass to hear Father Schettini preach eloquently in Italian.

Giuseppe Iannone and children in procession

Boys in St. Anthony Robes waiting for the procession to begin

St. Anthony Robes; 12 boys representing 12 Apostles
(Arthur Pallotta)

Anthony Paolino, Anthony Squizzero, Jerry Paolino, Antonio Cardi
(Barbara Palumbo)

Madeline Pallotta (Antonio Pallotta)

High Mass celebrated by Fr. Schettini

He was known as a great orator, and people came from near and far to hear him preach. After the procession and benediction, the community continued their feast, and people came from many states to celebrate this sacred day. An array of food, drink, and pastries were in abundance. One could hear the Italian music played by skilled musicians as they approached and passed the yards.

Serenade to Tina Cardi from Itri, at Conte home

Enrico and Tina Cardi from Itri. Enrico receiving the keys to the
City of Cranston from the former Mayor James Taft.

Mr. and Mrs. Americo Cardi and relatives hosting a reception for
Tina and Enrico Cardi from Itri.

It was a sight to behold as one witnessed and experienced the deep faith and joy the Itrani community created during this feast. One could visit any backyard or home and be welcomed on this special day.

As a child, I was impressed with the women who wore long black dresses and walked the length of the procession in bare feet, some on their knees. It was so hot, sometimes unbearable, but they continued with tongues parched from thirst. No one drank water. They wanted to sacrifice for the Madonna whom they believed would cure a sick one or help a family member or friend. They believed in penance and believed in miracles.

Our parish missions drew young and old alike. Often a hard message was delivered by the priest giving the mission. It seemed the fear of God was poured into us. We knew we had to walk a straight line. No one was really alone in Knightsville. Men and women watched out for neighbors' children, lest they would do something to disgrace the family or get into trouble. Most people lived in tenement houses.

Eviva Maria

Concetta and Marty Purificato in front of their store where all the neighborhood kids went for their candy, and other goodies.

Cosmo Capotosto and friend in front of Marty's Store

While many men gathered in front of Marty's store on Cranston Street to gossip and look out for the younger generation, the women would often sit outside, and their discussions would always be about family problems and the difficulties their friends and neighbors were experiencing. The community showed much concern over someone else's hardships, and much support and kindness was rendered to those that needed help. There was a strong bond with the immigrants who loved their homeland of Itri and often knew of each other's families and background. Although they lived with extreme hardships, they would share their food, homes, and listening ears to anyone, offering everything up to Jesus and Mary.

We never forgot what their life and upbringing was like for our parents in Itri. One could feel their longing to see their parents, family, and friends as they passionately talked of their families.

I am proud to say my roots stem from Itri, Italy, and my grandparents and parents gave me a heritage that no one can take away. The people from Itri had a mission, and they accomplished it well.

My intentions are not to exclude anyone or the facts that I am not aware of. Whatever I present is documented. I wanted our children and future generations to know the deep struggles, faith, and perseverance that our parents, grandparents, and ancestors experienced for us to be educated in our faith and to have a church in which we could worship freely without being persecuted because of our nationality or inability to communicate in the language of this country, as many other immigrants must have experienced when they arrived in America from their homelands.

Thirty eight years later, I'm completing the mission that was given to me by Reverend Andrew Farina in 1975. May Maria SS della Civita shower each of us with her graces now and forever.

Chapter 1
Itri and Immigration to a New Land

The town of Itri is situated in the valley of the Aurunci Mountains. It is 170 meters above sea level and measures 101.15 square kilometers in area. Itri is situated in the region of Lazio, whose province is Latina, and its population is 10,369. Itri is located 133 kilometers from Rome and 99 kilometers from Naples, respectively. It lies on the western coast of Italy, along the Tyrrhenian Sea.

The history of Itri can be traced back to the Roman Empire. The first road built by the Romans runs across the town, the Appian Way.

Old Appian Way

Some believe that Itri has roots as far back as the Etruscan period, and many speculate that the Etruscans were the engineers of the Appian Way, whereas the Romans benefited from their genius. Itri was a stopover rest area for the Roman garrison. Here they refreshed their mounts on the way to Naples.

Fountain of Gioacchino Murat in Itri

There are many hypotheses on the origin of the name *Itri*. Some believe that its name derives from *Iter*; the presence of an inscription on a block of stone found on the left-hand side of *Porta Mamurra* confirms this thesis.

Porta Mamurra (Joanne Merluzzo)

Others believe that it derived from the Latin word *atrium*, and yet others say it is a derivation of the same *Tar-it*, meaning "high ground." St. Maria is still referred to today as La Tarita. Another theory is that Itri derives from the work *Hydrus*, meaning "water serpent." This symbol is represented in the famous *Porta Mamurra* and is portrayed on the town crest, symbolizing health.

Porta Mamurra, stem of Itri (A. Saccoccio 1977)

Coat of arms of Itri, symbolizing health (Pecchia, 2003)

Others are inclined toward a more effective thesis—that of the presence of a rampant snake on Porta Mamurra. According to this thesis, the inhabitants of Amiclae fled from their land to seek refuge from an invasion of snakes, and so these were the real founders of Itri.

The focal point of Itri is the Medieval Castle. Probably built circa the tenth century, the castle is thirty-five meters in height. In recent years, it has been a subject of renovation and has been reopened to the public (Pecchia 2003).

Castle (Barbara Palumbo)

The people of Itri were not spared from the economic turmoil that occurred in Italy during the 1870s and 1880s. Abject poverty characterized the lifestyle of the lower classes throughout the country. The situation was due primarily to the semifeudal land system in which most acreage was owned by absentee aristocratic landlords. As in other European countries, family lots were divided and subdivided to descendants until virtually no opportunities remained for an individual to make ends meet.

The vast majority of people were so attached to their land that few thought of leaving permanently at first. Those who did leave in the early years were mostly males.

With American steamship company agents working out of nearly every village in Italy, it was not long before many more Italians made the choice to leave their homeland. American letters from newly arrived immigrants encouraged those who were hesitant to seize the opportunity. Some of the Itrani immigrants settled in Johnstown, Pennsylvania, and neighboring towns, where they worked on the railroad.

Itrani immigrants working on the railroad in Pennsylvania

They later settled in Cranston, Rhode Island forming their own community with those who had previously settled there.

The town of Cranston, with its present 80,529 inhabitants, was incorporated as a town in 1754. Italian immigrants settled in several Rhode Island neighborhoods, within the nearby city of Providence (Cranston). Just before the turn of the century, a group from Itri, in the province of Latina, settled in the Knightsville section of Cranston. They were people of diverse vocations—masons, bricklayers, unskilled manual laborers, and farmers—and brought with them their traditions and holiday celebrations. With the turn of the twentieth century, the number of Italians in Knightsville grew rapidly (Diocese of Providence).

Bernadette Conte

Immigrant workers at Budlong Farms in Cranston
(Cranston Historical Society)

Itri Square in Knightsville

The first and only Knightsville Reunion Organizing Committee; Frank Sinapi, Bernadette Conte, Frank Lepizzera and Lucy Altieri (not present in photo)
(Providence Journal, 2001)

Knightsville is named after local innkeeper and US congressman Nehemiah Knight (1746-1808). The Knights were descendants of early English immigrants who were some of the earliest settlers in the area. According to at least one source, Knightsville is known to some residents as Monkeytown, and Cranston Street leading to Knightsville is sometimes referred to as Monkeytown Road. One legend has it that a local lad joined a seafaring voyage, and when he returned, he brought back a most unusual creature with him—a monkey in a cage. People traveled from all over to see the animal. Monkeytown is hardly a respectable name for the community named after the Knight family, who owned much of the land in Knightsville and was dominant in state and local government (*wn.wikipedia.org/ wiki/talk:Knightsville*).

Although these newly arrived Italians brought few material possessions with them, they did possess a deep-seated faith and devotion to *their* Maria Santissima della Civita.

Chapter 2
Maria Santissima della Civita

The sanctuary and the painting of the Civita share a millenary history. The folk tradition narrate that a deaf and dumb shepherd found the holy image while he was in search of one of his lost cows in the bushes of Mount Civita. It was among the branches of a holm oak tree where the cow was kneeling, and in that moment, the shepherd regained his voice and hearing.

Miracle on Mt. Civita (Lombardini, 1976)

This is how the history and the Civitana devotion begin. The origins of this painting and how it got to us are a mystery, being that the place was so inaccessible.

The sacred image is said to date back to the iconoclast persecutions of Constantinople, which were inflicted by the emperor Leone Isaurico, in about the eighth century AD.

It is said that at that time, two Brazilian monks were caught with the image and were locked in a chest with the painting and then thrown into the sea. Their voyage ended fifty-four days later in Messina on the Sicilian coast. Here, for the first time, the picture was exhibited so that it could be venerated by the local faithful.

The history of *our* Madonna starts with its disappearing from Messina and its being found on Mount Civita. Many authors believed that St. Luke the Evangelist was the author of this picture because the presence of three letters, now practically vanished, placed on the base of the picture (Michel Angelo Di Arezzo, *Historia* 1633): LMP, which stands for "Lucas Me Pinxit."

Sacred image of the Madonna della Civita
painted by St. Luke

Antique Painting protected by a grate

Pope Pius 1X (Lombardini 1976)

Among the many authors consulted with regard to these subject matters, the best version is that of Don Michele Colaquori, who aroused a certain interest that went beyond the sacredness of the image (Pecchia 2003).

The more likely story that we can imagine is that of the Brazilian monks who, passing by in this area and landing in Gaeta, must have left the painting of excellent oriental manufacture to the monks of the Figline Monastery.

There is a historical certainty that dates back to 1147, in which there is reference to a small church called Madonna della Civita. One of these documents states that in 1147, a notary from Itri and his wife made a donation. The document carries the signature of a certain Richard, abbot of the monastery, and that Father Bartolomeo was the caretaker of the little church. Thus, historically speaking, this is the most reliable source from which to start, briefly, the account of the events that distinguished the life of the sanctuary and to talk about the image of the Civita.

The Civita millennium was solemnly commemorated with celebration that conveyed the faithful, the religious, and the civil authorities to the sanctuary from May 27-31, 2000, in order to recall the thousand-year devotion to Mary. The height of the ceremonies was the Theological Pastoral Convention and the solemn liturgical celebration, an oriental Catholic rite. It would be impossible to name all the renowned pilgrims that visited or stayed at the sanctuary because there were so many.

February 10, 1849, Pope Pius 1X
at the altar of the Civita (Lombardini 1976)

A PIO IX
CHE IL 10 FEBBRAIO 1849
8 GIORNI DOPO LA PUBBLICAZIONE
DELL'ENCICLICA UBI PRIMUM
VENNE A PREGARE LA VERGINE
E DI QUA TRAEVA CONFORTO
PER DEFINIRLA IMMACOLATA
IL DI 8 DICEMBRE 1854
IL POPOLO ITRANO
FESTEGGIANDO L'ANNO CINQUANTESIMO
DELLA PROCLAMAZIONE SOSPIRATA DA SECOLI
P.P.

Pope Pius 1X, and plaque in his memory (Lombardini 1976)

FERDINANDUS II
UTRIUSQUE SICILIÆ ATQUE JERUSALEM REX
FRANCISCUS ALOISIUS ET ALPHONSUS FILII
FRANCISCUS DE PAULA FRATER
BINAEQUE SORORES KAROLINA ET MARIA AMALIA
CUM HUJUS CONJUGE SEBASTIANO HISPANIARUM INFANTE
PRO ANTIQUA DOMUS REGIÆ IN VIRGINEM PIETATE
ET RELIGIOSA ERGA APOSTOLICAM SEDEM VENERATIONE
PONTIFICI PIO IX LITANTI
ECCLESIAM ET REGNUM UT DEUS SERVET INCOLUMES
PRAESIDIUM VIRGINIS PRECANTES ADSTITERE
NE ITAQUE UNQUAM OBLIVIOSA AETAS
TANTA AEDIS HUJUS RELIGIOSA DECORA OBLITERET
POSTERITATEM ISTHAEC MONIMENTA DOCENT

King Ferdinando 11 (Lombardini 1976)

St. Paolo della Croce, 1726 (Lombardini 1976)

Plaque in memory of St. Paolo della Croce (Lombardini 1976)

The most important famous people known were Pope Pius IX, who came on February 10, 1849, together with King Ferdinand II and the royal family; St. Filippo Nero, who came in 1532; St. Paolo della Croce in 1726; B. Paolo Burali d'Arezzo, who was born in Itri and later became bishop of Piacenza and cardinal of Naples; St. Leonardo da Porto Maurizio, who stayed there for quite a while in 1772; St. Gaspare del Bufalo in 1824; St. Maria De Mattias, founder of the Preziosissimo Sangua nuns (and while she was there, comforted by the advice given her by St. Gaspare and the canon servant of God, Giuseppe Addessi, she found her definite vocation); and the Cardinal Montini, who came on January 25, 1935, before he was raised to the papal seat of Pietro with the name of Paolo VI. In the church courtyard, a memorial stone can be seen right beside the portico, on which names of saints, the blessed, the venerable, and other important people who came there in prayer have been quoted.

It was in 1491 that from a little church, the sanctuary started to acquire its actual characteristic features. The citizens of Itri pressed the bishop of Gaeta to have a bigger church. They were not only contented with a church, but Monsignor Francesco Patrizi emitted a consecrated bull, in which he wished to hand down to future descendants the effort made by the people of Itri by writing, "*Praecipue ducti precibus universitatis et hominum terrae Itri.*" Furthermore, he wrote, "*De iure administrazionis et patronatus dictae universitatis eiusdem ecclesiae.*" The following year, in a further document, he confirmed that the men of the land of Itri were the founders, patrons, and supporters of the sanctuary. In the same bull on June 20, 1491, when talking about the picture, he underlined the continuous veneration for the sanctuary and for the picture of the Madonna, calling it antique venerations. The bull, which Monsignor Patrizi extends to his descendants, is the most important document present in this holy place. In 1775, during his supplication, Monsignor Pergamo, bishop of Gaeta, made reference to the antiquity of the picture and to the often-visited sanctuary in order to plea the Vatican an authorization for a solemn coronation of the virgin that successfully took place later on July 21, 1777. It was Pentecost Monday when the church was inaugurated in the presence of the whole clergy community and the people of Itri, and since then, it has undergone various restorations during the course of centuries. Confiding in the devotion and support that the faithful would have given, it was thought that with time the church could be enlarged and provided with rooms to host pilgrims.

The first stone of today's structure was blessed on May 27, 1820, and works finished in 1828. On February 25, 1849, fifteen days after Pius IX visited the sanctuary, the cardinal Gabriele Ferretti inaugurated the church. And it was Pope Pius IX who, in 1877, signed the decree for the second coronation, *a grace that is by no means ordinary but is not sufficiently justified,* answered the pope to those who made the request; however, he later granted it, remembering the visit he had made to the Civita. For this second great occasion, a commemorative medal was coined, that I would never have thought of finding in the home of my relative in Fondi.

July 20, 1877, 2nd Coronation of Madonna della Civita (Lombardini, 1976)

Coin in memory of the Coronation (Pecchia2003)

Park of music July 21, 1952 where the benediction took place before the Madonna departed for the *santuario*. (L. Marcella- Royal Crown Copyright)
Pat Maggiacomo

On the left side of the sanctuary, there is a headstone in memory of Pope Pius IX, who had paused in one of the pavilion rooms during his visit together with the exiled king Ferdinand II. The pope's gifts were some sacred vestments (still under sanctuary custody), a silver goblet, and ten gold coins.

Silver goblet given by Pope Pius 1X (Lombardini 1976)

A parchment that has gone yellow with age carries the inscription, written by his hand, "*Gloriosa dicta sunt de Te, Civitas Dei. Die decima febbraio 1849. PP. IX.*"

And even the king's visit left its signs. This kind of event is considered of great importance for such places because, on this particular occasion, the king had ordered that a carriageway be built in order to connect the *Ciociaria* area to Itri and Itri to be linked to the port of Gaeta, which was only seven kilometers away. To reach the sanctuary, the pope and the king had ridden on horseback along the ancient mule track that was evidenced by the Stations of the Cross chapels.

Today we can comfortably reach the sanctuary along the SS 82 Valle del Liri road. It was a deed not of little count for the population and for commercial links of those times (Pecchia 2003).

CHAPTER 3
Visit to the Sanctuary

Driving along the state road that unwinds through a holm oak forest, one reaches the sanctuary on the top of a hillock, where cars and buses, which are always plentiful, can find an ample parking area.

Santuario of the Maria SS. della Civita (Pecchia 2003)

All around, one can admire the daisy-covered meadows, where once the pilgrims used to picnic after having attended the religious function.

The atmosphere is reduced to the bare essentials; for this, we can thank the fathers, who alternated one another in guiding the sanctuary, and the municipal administrator, who protected the area from any type of commercial exploitation. This place of silence and faith is free from mobile relief centers and vendors of any type. However, for those who prefer it, there is a bar-restaurant run by a private citizen, especially during the summertime or on major festivities. Religiosity and silence are a rule in this place of faith.

Climbing up the stairway, on the right hand side, one can enter rooms that are occupied by the manger scene and memorial plaques left by those who made promises for graces received and a small trade market selling souvenirs, which is run by the Passionist priests, to whom the responsibility of this pious place has been entrusted.

Plaques in Miracle Room in thanksgiving for miracles received.

Padre Francesco Vaccelli in miracle and souveneir room

Padre Francesco in the *santuario*

Bernadette Conte's visit to the *santuario* and Padre Francesco Vaccelli

Father Cherubino di Feo, a man not easily forgotten who was once parish priest in Itri's church and St. Maria Maggiore, is now retired to the sanctuary, where he not only carries out his priestly duties, but he also constantly researches on information about such places; and it is for this reason that he can be considered the historical memory of the sanctuary.

Proceeding to the top of the stairway and passing under the bell tower, on the left, one can find the memorial stone that was unveiled on June 26, 1990, by Monsignor Vincenzo M. Farano, at the time archbishop of Gaeta, in memory of the visit made by Pope Giovanni Paolo II on June 25, 1989.

Memorial Plaque in memory of Pope Giovanni Paolo 11

Upon it lean other building works that are necessary to the everyday life of the priests and the many collaborators, who come daily from Itri and other surrounding towns (Fondi, Formia, Gaeta, and Sperlonga) in order to help the priests during the religious functions and in all the primary activities needed in the daily conduction of life at the Civita. The priests consider these activities of great importance, especially the effort made by the collaborators toward the thousands of faithful who come to the Civita during the whole year.

I would like to recall a document that belongs to Bishop Patrizi, in which he granted spiritual privileges to visitors and pilgrims. It also quotes the phrase "*manusque adjutrices pergentibus*" in talking about the volunteers of the sanctuary, to whom he lavishly gave as reward spiritual advantages. After 512 years, their efforts are still noteworthy (Pecchia 2003).

CHAPTER 4
The Church

The church is made up of three aisles, the central one being wider than the two side aisles, which are rather narrow. The high altar at the center of the nave is of particular interest. It is made of marble and marquetry belonging to Neapolitan School (1700); the master Mr. Filippo Pecorella made the works. The decorations on the vault, which portray some of the events that characterize the birth of the sanctuary and the events that followed, were carried out by Mr. S. Cozzolino from Naples in 1919. They were later restructured by the professor A. Rollo from Bari, the sculptor who carved the Madonna that is placed at the external top of the church. To complete the two side aisles, each has an altar; on the left is the altar dedicated to St. Gioacchino, and on the right, to St. Anne. The balustrade that surrounds the high altar is beautiful and rich in precious marquetry. The two columns of the altar come from the convent of St. Francesco in Itri, as well as the wash basin found in the sacristy. The painting of the Madonna of the Civita is placed at the center of the high altar and is protected by a crystal glass pane.

Pope Giovanni Paolo 11 kneeling at altar of the *santuario*
(Arture Mari, D.D. De Meo 2002)

To complete the church furniture, there is a wooden choir belonging to the eighteenth century and a pipe organ. In a small room, so-called *tesoro* (treasure), are kept precious objects and sacred vestments that were donated by famous faithful and pilgrims, one of whom was Pope Pius IX. Kept in custody here, there are some canvases of valuable make—a *Nativity* of Neapolitan School, a *Madonna with St. Francesco from Paola Neapolitan School and the Assumption*, along with a copy of the *Madonna of the Civita* on wood, which is considered by experts to be of noteworthy value; these three paintings are said to be the work of Sebastiano Conca from Gaeta (1680-1764), a painter of excellent skill who came to the sanctuary to recover from a bad illness; it is said that besides painting the three above-mentioned works, he had retouched the miraculous picture of the Civita.

So this is the sanctuary, a place of prayer, an oasis of peace between heaven and earth. The message of hope is strong—a hope that is sustained by genuine faith—and the pilgrims, both famous and not, receive this message. They have been coming to this sacred place for a thousand years to find themselves before the virgin of the Civita, who bestows her grace. Just as she had done back in 1527 when Itri's population was decimated by an epidemic of pestilence and in turning to their faith, *the painting was taken in procession through the streets of the town. In the meantime, the people implored that the infectious disease would come to an end. Suddenly during this function, they saw a cloud lift from the ground, and it dissipated in the air. A few moments from then, the disease came to an end.* In memory of this event, the date established to celebrate annually the Civita, and her first crowning was July 21 (Pecchia 2003).

CHAPTER 5
The Miraculous Picture

The image found on Mount Civita is of Byzantine style.

July 14, 2002—The Rector P. Renato Santilli, with the Mayor of Itri Giovanni Agresti, at the celebration of the sacred image. (Pecchia 2003)

During the course of the centuries, very little is left of the ancient features (claimed to be St. Luca's); the picture has undergone restoration more than once. With certainty, Conca Senior did one at the end of 1600, and Mr. Pandozzi did the other on the occasion of the first coronation in 1777. The technique used by Mr. Pandozzi was that of substituting the ancient tablet with a copper plate, and then he restored the canvas. In 1815, a strike of lightning hit the image, risking the destruction of the canvas. So it was placed on a wooden frame after having removed the copper plate, and in this way, the picture has reached our days.

The most important restoration was carried out by the late professor Edelwais Frezzan in 1953. It was from him that I (Pino Pecchia) learned how he actually carried out the operation, and the following is quoted from his report published on June 30, 1953: *"Due to the humidity, I thought it necessary to apply a double lining of wax to the painting, according to the techniques adopted in paintings of the northern countries, assuring in this way a more or less eternal preservation,* warning that *if in the future, for whatever reason, someone should have to carry out further works of restoration, he should take strong count of what I have detailed in this report."*

On March 18, 2002, Pino Pecchia received news from the priests of the sanctuary saying that the picture had been taken to a restoration center in Rome, called Koinè, and it had undergone radiography, stratigraphy, and other laboratory processing; and the rumors, which in the past stated that there was a presence of figures overlapping the image due to the various restorations, have resulted groundless. What is certain is that there are traces of color that outline some parts of the body, but these traces are totally absent on the facial area. The picture has undergone cleaning because of the presence of scratches and holes in places where, in 1777, the crown had been fixed. April 19, 2002, was the twenty-fifth anniversary of when the image was brought to Itri on the occasion of the bicentenary of the first coronation of the Madonna (1777).

Year of the Jubilee

On the occasion of the bicentenary celebration of the coronation that took place for the first time in 1777, the committee, being unable to add a third crown to the image, decided to invite the pope to the solemn religious celebrations by writing an invitation to the Vatican secretariat of state, asking his presence at the ceremony:

> "*The members of the Organizing Committee of the celebration in honor of Holy Mary of the Civita, on occasion of the bicentenary of the coronation of Her venerated image, united with the Rector Father of the Guanelliani monks of the above mentioned Sanctuary and the Reverend Parish Priest of the Passionist Monks of the A. G. P. parish in Itri, place where the celebrations usually take place after those that take first place at the Sanctuary, and after preventive agreements taken with our Archbishop in Gaeta, Monsignor Luigi Maria Carli, humbly permit themselves to send trustful petition to this Secretariat of State of His Holiness, in order that the Holy Father Paolo VI kindly grants to the church of Gaeta, the joy of having His generous and personal presence here in Itri at the Sanctuary* [possibly within the period July 17-24, 1977] *presence that will be highly significant to this organization and will arouse deep and noble sentiments of love to the Mother of God and to the Supreme Shepherd of the Church of Jesus Christ. With faith and humility we shall. pray to our Lady of the Civita who once gave to Pius IX courage and light in those difficult moments for the church, should today give to our beloved Pope Paolo VI new energy to guide Christ's church in these times that are probably more difficult than they were. We dare in hoping to obtain such a grace and, while we express to this Secretariat of State of His Holiness our deepest devotion and gratitude, permit ourselves to ask from you your apostolic blessings.*"

Signed
The President Father Alberto Rivezzi

The committee ordered the jeweler, Mr. Petrillo from Itri, to make a decorative element in gold and semiprecious stones so that they could be fixed to the base of the two crowns of the Madonna (seven sapphires of, 19, 75 karats and 59, 6 grams of gold 750 × 1000). This jewel, which was made free of charge, would be a token in remembrance of the great recurrence for future generations. A sapphire was also placed on the child's forehead. Officiated by the cardinal Vagnozzi, the "crown" was placed at the base of the existing ones. This does not mean that it was a third crowning, like some writers had erroneously published after the event. What the eminent event was really about can be read in Mr. Orazio La Rocca's introductory "brochure," edited by me (Pecchia 2003).

The whole event was framed by hundreds of faithful followers who came from the various surrounding regions to venerate the sacred image. The encounter between the late ex-mayor Mr. Pasquale Ciccone and Itri's immigrants, who came from various towns of the USA, was very touching, and there were moments of profound sentiments during the days that preceded the actual celebration.

Sisters: Gaetanina Cardi Capotosto, and Maria Civita Cardi Longo attending feast in Itri, 1977. (E. Cardi)

Group from Cranston, R. I. (Knightsville) attending feast in Itri, 1977 (E. Cardi)

Plaque in Itri in remembrance of the people of Cranston

This union was strengthened by the dedication of the day to their honor. Not only the USA immigrants funded the celebrations, but the Canadian immigrants also gave a conspicuous sum.

The participants to the religious ceremony were the cardinal Vagnozzi, the bishop Costantini from Sessa Aurunca, the bishop Compagnone from Terracina, the abbot Matronola from Montecasino, and the archbishop Carli from Gaeta. There were many civil and literary authorities from the nearby towns and provinces. The religious ceremonies were highlighted by encounters and musical shows (the state police band from the towns of Mottola and Lecce, the choir from Latina, the singer Mr. Peppino Gagliardi, the groups the Romans and July & Julye, the Perez Prado show, and the jazz orchestra of the sixth fleet of the NATO forces) and a number of events, including the first Olive Festival.

Gianpaolo Cardi and women of Itri sorting olives

News of the celebration was broadcasted on a closed circuit by the local transmitting television, RTBL from Formia, enabling the elderly and the sick of Itri to watch and follow the happenings of this long-awaited event directly from their homes.

I consider this event a very dear one because I was personally involved in the organization, and I shall always keep in mind that nostalgic memory. I shall also keep deep in my heart the memory of the late Father Alberto Rivezzi, who was the president of the committee and the parish of St. Maria Maggiore. He was a master of faith and life (Pecchia 2003).

Santa Maria Maggiore Church, Itri

July 13, 2002, arrival of the sacred image at the Square
of the Coronation, Itri (Pecchia 2003)

Chapter 6

Rescue of the Madonna

During World War II, 75 percent of Itri was destroyed. Residents left their homes and ran to the hill country, hiding from the German soldiers. Fathers feared for their daughters and did all they could from having their daughters and wives raped. We have all heard horror stories through members of our families and friends of what the Itrani population and many others endured during these trying times. They had little food or material possessions as they ran to hide in the caves of the hill country. Their homes were destroyed with the bombings, and Itri had to be rebuilt. My own paternal grandfather, Ornorato Capotosto, who refused to leave his home, was killed in the bombardment of Itri. The Itrani immigrants waited daily for news of their families, not knowing if they were still living.

During the invasion of the German soldiers, the rector of the sanctuary, Don Lidio Borgese, hid the painting under his cloak, passing through Cisterna, Sonninno, and the Lepini Mounts as he ran from the Germans. Don Lidio writes:

> April 22, 1944, Sonnino
>
> Having read the letter, I decided to respond out of respect to authority and to show all my good negative reasons. The following day, a woman came to listen to mass.
>
> "*I bring you the English.*" This pious woman came down the mountain while the twenty-four four-engine planes went daily towards Anzio and Cassino and bombed this part of the country that had not been previously included in the hostility. The victims were numerous, the panic substantial. The Blessed Mother saved us again. It became like this in the first half of the month of May the happiness that we felt at the retreat was disturbed by the screams and cries that we heard one evening. Some women who had come from a neighbor's house announced to us that two fugitive Germans, not being able to find

Eviva Maria

one of their comrades, believed that they had been killed by one of us. They vowed then and there that they would destroy every home with hand grenades. Without wasting any time, we took the Madonna and went down the valley. That was at 8:00 and we arrived close to 10:00, suffering such torments that only God knows. Someone that we knew offered us something to eat, but we refused everything. Going without food is not more painful than suffering. I lay down on a bed specifically prepared for me, but not even a half hour had passed that the sound of the cannons began again. The first shot from the artillery from the offensive fell 150 meters from the little house where we were. I woke up in a hurry and asked the image of the Madonna, "*What is happening in our land?*" We arrived at a farmhouse hidden between trees where we stayed for the entire night praying in the middle of so many evacuees. The fire fight lasted until five in the morning. Given the nature of the departure, I pointed out the goal that we would try to reach, the place near the mountain on the opposite side of the valley. We began with plenty of faith on our ascent up the mountain while the bombardment assailed us from the fall of Terracina. Cannonballs and bombs fell about three kilometers from us. Those that fell on Sonnino, I believe, were no farther than 500 meters away. I lifted the painting of the Madonna to bless the land on which I saw cannons landing, giving peace to the dead and calming the living.

While I was climbing, praying, blessing, and sighing, I heard the voice of a woman calling to me that said, "*Father, come up, everything that was said yesterday is not true. Give the Madonna to me and the baggage, I will help you.*"

Walking a few more steps, a farmer came closer to me and said, "*Don Lidio, we have been told that the Americans are at the Monte delle Fate. They have advised us all to remain inside and to hide the animals, because at three, they would pass by here.*"

I accelerated my pace in order to reach the humble room that was waiting for me, and after a modest meal, I lay down on the bed. The inside door could not be closed. In order to fix this, I put a chair in front of it. Not even ten minutes after I lay down, confused voices woke me from my half slumber. Suddenly, the chair fell to the ground and the door opened wide. A young woman, half dressed, and her hair in disarray entered, and announced to me the arrival of the Americans were less than two kilometers away.

Astonished, I watched her while with a noble simplicity, [she] said to me, "*Father, I bring you the English. Come to see.*" After about thirty meters of street, we saw a column of about three thousand men. I thanked everyone and returned to the peace of my rest.

American Soldiers in Itri. (WW 11 archives)

But my trepidations were not yet finished. The Germans tried to bring war to their enemies and they went down into the nearby valleys. They were little centers that the fantasies of our farmers announced to us like divisions. Out of fear, they planned to depart the following day. We traversed on foot all of the mountains from the Croce de Sonnino to the Monte delle Fate. We descended this last one and arrived at the lower slope mountain. There were signs of a patrol of Americans following the Germans. We walked on hands and knees. The poor young boy that had followed me voiced concern, "*Don Lidio, move to the pulping mill.*" I said to him, "*Don't be afraid, we have the Madonna della Civita with us.*" At the middle of our descent, we found a donkey who would carry our baggage. Slowly, we arrived at the place that was called "Serra dell Palomba." Here, my heart expanded. Suddenly, to my eyes appeared the plains of Fondi, in the background of the sky was Monte Ruazzo, which meant sanctuary. The house of the Madonna was in walking distance, although far away. She was with me like when she was with the two religious men who needed to reach their home. A tumult of feeling hit my heart, and in my mind, I began to repeat verses of poetry.

While I was repeating these verses from memory, the man who was leading the donkey told me that the journey was finished. The woman carried the painting of the Madonna on her head and didn't want to put it down until she reached Monte S. Biagio.

I rested, worn out, in the vicinity of this land where the hardworking Americans got into a jeep and took us, making their way to Itri. When I saw this little city in the condition that today the traveler can admire, I had a stab of pain in my heart. It was the first time that I saw the scourge of God that we call war.

Bombardment of Itri (Don Virgilio Mancini)

Don Virgilio Mancini friend to Gaetanina and Reverend Roland Cardi. (M. Cardi Barone)

Don Virgilio Mancini (M.Cardi Barone)

The Administrator of the sanctuary wanted to keep me inside because the Moroccans were in the mountains. I stayed there for approximately three days in his house, and then, I preferred to go up and down from the sanctuary in order to get supplies to begin the work of restoration of the building and of the adoration" (Sac. Ignazio Lombardini 1976).

2 German soldiers carrying injured soldiers Itri, 1944. (WW11 archives)

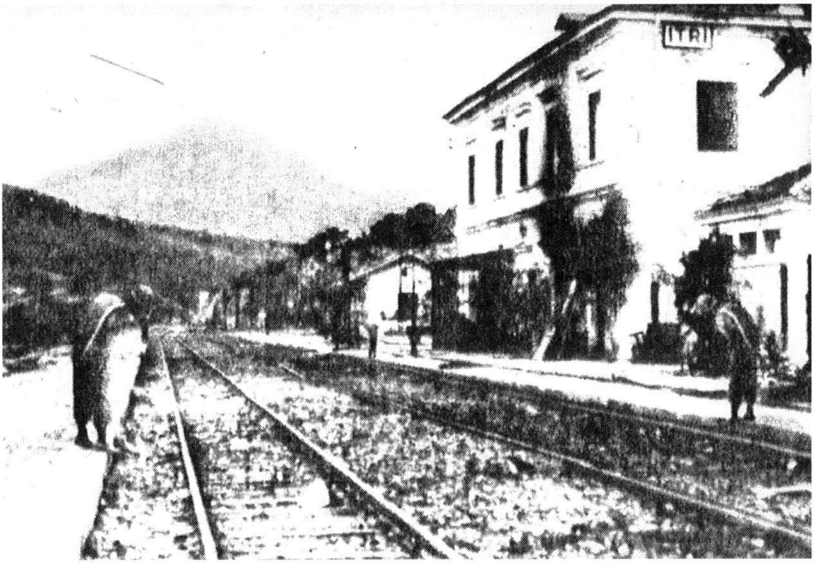
ITRI

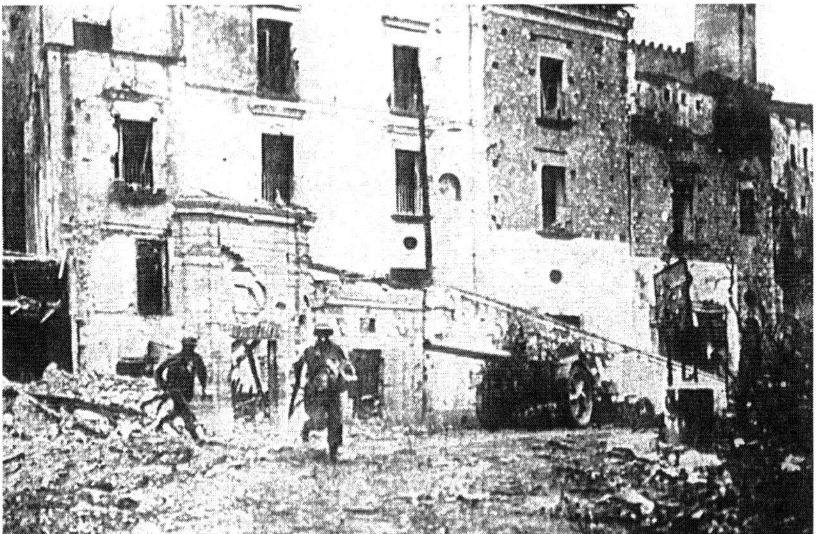

Bombardment, and rescue of Itri by American soldiers, 1944 (WW11 archives)

Chapter 7
The Silver Statue

"*The year 1840, on the second day of the month of August, the reigning king, Ferdinand II, of the reign of the Two Sicilies, by the grace of God*"—this is how the deed and the history of the silver statue of the Madonna of the Civita started. The work of art was demanded by the notable people of Itri, who collected the necessary sum of money to pay for the casting, which, among other expenses, totalized the sum of 828 ducati and 30 grana, added to the cost of registering procedure in Fondi's office in book 1, volume 39 on page 91, and the recipient being Mr. Paolo D'Ettore.

The statue weighs thirty-six pounds eleven ounces. Both the *Madonna and Child* wear a gold-plated copper crown with precious stones of various shades, and the whole statue is covered with 130 golden stars.

Bernadette Conte

Feast in Itri, 2013 (Stephanie Stabile)

The donors were 326, but they were not only from Itri but also from Castellone (Formia), Gaeta, Fondi, and the church of St. Maria Assunta in Cielo. Many of them were anonymous and preferred not to be quoted in the deed. There were donations also from the fair of the Civita feast. These spontaneous and anonymous donations make one's mind reflect. The subscription for the collection of the money necessary lasted a long time, as results from the inscription behind the statue, which was cast in 1839, and the deed was stipulated in August 1840. So to affirm that the heirs of the donors are today the owners of the statue could only have a legal logic. If, instead, we analyze the contents of the deed, we realize that the names of the people quoted had acted on behalf of third parties, and thus, they cannot be considered heirs. On one of the deeds that carry only names without references to personal data makes it impossible to identify anyone, except for the church of St. Maria Assunta in Cielo, the St. Martino Monastery, and other names belonging to well-off families that are easily identifiable. The veneration that the people of Itri had toward the icon of the Madonna of the Civita before—and successively, to *their* silver statue—is common to all.

The birth of the association was one of the wisest decisions taken by the people of Itri of today. The inventors of the subscription and its consequent deed gave to all the "devout" rich and poor donors, anonymous and occasional, the possibility to make that statue. It seems to me to be quite un-Christian-like, toward that "public of Itri" quoted in the deed, to suppose voluntarily any discrimination toward the poverty of the many people who could not contribute at that time. Thus, the statue does not belong to the Commune of Itri as institution but to its people. It is clear that the will of this community, today as it was in the past, is that each year they hold the celebration in July with the procession of *their* statue.

Once upon a time, it was kept in custody by the noble family called De Fabritis, right up to the beginning of the 1990s, but after doubtful and unrespectable happenings, this commitment was revoked by a writ of the magistrate; thus, it was kept in custody by the police for a brief period of time. Then for a couple of years, it was kept in an armor room of the commune buildings. Rumors had said that some of the treasures, like gold objects that had been donated by the faithful during the course of years, were found at a pawnbroker in Rome. After a general mobilization and various legal procedures, a solution was found, and it satisfied everyone. The statue was placed at the end of the left nave of the church St. Maria Maggiore, well protected from ill-intentioned people, with a crystal glass pane and a grating. This seemed to be the best solution, at least for that moment. So the people of Itri can at any time have the possibility to pray and ask for graces from their Madonna.

The engineer Mr. La Rocca designed the chapel in which it stands. Mario La Rocca and the artist Mrs. Florentine Wallner planned the stained-glass window.

Going back to that mobilization about the disappearing of the gold treasures, I'd like to mention that the Association of Holy Mary came to being with a deed under the seal of a notary, and it was not by chance that the naming of the two heads were both representatives of two different generations. This can be considered an ideal connection to the famous deed stipulated in Naples far back on August 1840. The honorary chairman the association named was Mr. Fausto Saccoccio, nicknamed Faustino, who had been the president of the Civita Celebrations Committee for decades; the responsible chairman named was Mr. Orazio La Rocco, a Vatican journalist of the daily newspaper *La Repubblica*, and he represents the new generations.

The association can be considered an ideal baton that the people of Itri have today once again proposed—a baton to strengthen and hand down to the future generation the ideals of their fathers who wanted to evince with this silver statue casting their most genuine expression of popular faith. The finality of the association is that of voluntary service. The members are the lawyer Mr. Antonio Fargiorgio (VP), the engineer Mr. Mario La Rocca, the teacher Mr. Mimmo Del Bove, Mr. Mimmo Fabrizio, Ms. Maria Maggiacomo, the actual mayor of Itri, and the parish priest of St. Maria Maggiore. The auditors—Mr. Peppino De Santis, Mr. Luigi Saccoccio and Mr. Giovanni Nofi—are the guarantors of the technical bookkeeping sector.

There are cultural meetings and photographic exhibitions, which started in 2003 and will continue on, with the aim of finding photographic and illustrated material that can document the cult toward the Virgin of the Civita during the past centuries. There is also a competition, proposed to the schools of Itri, which aims in regaining the historical memory of the Civita. The young students' duty is to collect information from their grandparents and parents about live evidence of faith, which could otherwise be lost in time, strengthening the inseparable bond that thousands of years have tied the people of Itri to the Madonna of the Civita (Pecchia 2003).

CHAPTER 8
Visit of Pope Giovanni Paolo II

June 25, 1989, marks an important stage for the sanctuary's history. The pope Karol Wojtyla came in pastoral visit to the archdiocese of Gaeta; the sanctuary was also in the itinerary for the meeting of the sick.

Pope Giovanni Paolo 11 arrival on Mt. Civita (Pecchia)

Pope Giovanni Paolo 11 greeted by Fr. Giuseppe Polselli
(Sac. Govanni De Meo 2002)

The pope arrived by helicopter and landed on an open space where once stood the Convent of the Figline nuns. The foreign minister Mr. Giulio Andreotti, the bishop Vincenzo M. Farano, and the mayor of Itri, Mr. Pasquale Ciccone, welcomed him. The encounter with the sick at the sanctuary of the Civita was a moment that signed both heart and mind of all those present. His Holiness's hand that caresses the sick and the sweetness in which he speaks to them with words full of hope will always remain impressed in the minds of all the participants to the event.

The greetings of the mayor, Mr. Ciccone (who died prematurely), followed those of the pope Giovanni Paolo II, which were profound and meaningful. And not withstanding their physical disabilities, the sick drew from those words of comfort and hope, and in welcoming the pope, they prayed with the following words: "*We ask you to increase our faith so that we can live with our sufferings as a sharing of the life and passion of Jesus Christ.*" And here everyone was overcome by emotion. The ceremony with the sick had been preceded by a visit to the church. The pope was received in the church courtyard by the passionate community, led by the general superior, Father Jose Augustin Orbegozo; by the provincial superior, Father Giuseppe Comparelli; and by the rector of the sanctuary, Father Giusepppe Polselli. He paused to admire the floral picture produced by the floral artists of Itri. It was a delicate composition of rose, carnation, and field flower petals portraying both the Vatican and Itri's coat of arms, the pope's face, and some of Itri's important monuments.

A carpet of flowers for Pope Giovanni Paolo 11 made by artists. (Pecchia 2003)

He then knelt before the high altar in prayer toward the miraculous effigy of the Civita. There were moments of silence, concentration gently broken by the hum of about one thousand faithful waiting out in the open space of the sanctuary. It was a historical day for the Civita and for its few faithful, including all the civil and military authorities of Itri, the latter being admitted to the ceremony for safety reasons. The atmosphere, already impregnated with high spirituality both for the place and for the presence of Christ's vicar, became practically surreal when a blanket of mist covered everyone for a few moments. It was June 25, 1989, a sunny and clear day, but due to that sudden phenomenon, a particular atmosphere came to being, and in that moment, the heavens seemed to be within reach (Pecchia 2003).

CHAPTER 9
The 225th Anniversary of the Crowning of the Madonna

While the sun's splendid golden-colored rays were setting amid the sloping hills of the land of Itri, in the distance, echoing through the valley, were the sounds—hardly audible but getting closer—of melodious voices belonging to devoted people uttering their prayers and songs toward the heavens, glorifying their Virgin Mary. Sweet songs of ancient memories that narrate of an icon that came from far away. So it was, thousands of years ago, that those faithful followers who first saw the icon, quite different from today's one, referred to the holy image as the brunette Madonna of the Civita from Constantinople.

It was July 14, 2002. The holy icon of the Civita descended to Itri, carried on careful shoulders, in turn, through an ancient rocky pathway down the hillside, which had been ridden down on horseback back in 1849 by Pius IX.

Men carrying the Madonna from the *santuario* to town of Itri.
(Salvatore Marcini)

Even though 1902-2001 is not a centenary, in 1902, the first twenty-fifth anniversary of Our Lady being carried down on shoulders by the people of Itri was celebrated, and that year was the 225th anniversary since the first crowing; five are the recurrences on which the holy image has come down from her throne to meet her children.

Procession into town of Itri (Pat Maggiacomo)
(Marcello-Royal Crown copyright 1952)

One hundred years would have been too many, but twenty-five years were just right to recall that far back on July 21, 1527, to watch the sacred icon cross every corner of the town.

The population hands down from generation to generation that when the *tetra maligna caligine* dissipated, putting an end to the plague that raged Itri, thanks to her intercession through her divine son. They should pay tribute to the Virgin Mary, dedicating to her this day for the miracle received.

Her feast day started right there in her home, the Sanctuary of the Civita, a place of prayer dedicated to her, an oasis of peace between heaven and earth—destination, in past centuries, for saints and for the blessed, for the powerful and for simple devout, all kneeling before her and imploring celestial grace.

It was just in the same way that this 225th anniversary started. She appeared at the top of the flight of stairs that led down to Piazzale Don Lidio Borgese; a rejoicing population, who have come to take her and have her in Itri for ten days, exploded into a rousing ovation, followed by hymns to her, dedicated during the passing of centuries. She was placed on the right-hand side of the altar, which had been prepared outdoors. The provincial Passionist superior, Father P. Stanislao Renzi, along with the rector, Father Renato Santilli, and other members of the confraternity, officiated the Eucharistic celebration. The Mother of God was at the center of the homily directed at over a thousand people who crowded the large square—the obedience of a humble handmaid, designated by God to redeem mankind through her son, Jesus. There was a blessing to all those children who had come to take the Mother of all, so-called Civita, and with these words ended the opening ceremony awaited for twenty-five years.

Indescribable and not even quantifiable was the number of people present at Raino locality to meet the sacred image. The program planned by the committee and religious authorities of Itri was completely upset. The Eucharistic celebration, due to start at nine o'clock, only started at eleven o'clock.

They had to walk for two hours a little more than a kilometer.

girls dressed as angels (Pat Maggiacomo)
(Marcello-Royal Crown copyright 1952)

Madonna arrives at Santa Maria Maggiore
(Pat Maggiacomo-Royal Crown Copyright 1952)

There were young girls dressed as angels, children and elderly women wearing ancient Itri costumes, a horseman wearing an epoch uniform, who led the procession, a multicolored and numerous groups of emigrants who came just for the occasion from the USA; and little Canadian flags waved happily by the Itri community from Toronto—all to escort the image, which was placed on a flowered throne.

The rector, Santilli, symbolically handed over to Itri's mayor the image of the Madonna of the Civita, a gesture not at all without meaning. Relating all these things makes the mind go back in times long gone to a bull issued by the bishop Monsignor Patrizi in 1491; it said, "*Praecipue ducti precibus universitatis et hominum terrae Itri*," meaning that the bishop of Gaeta recognized Itri and its people to be the "founders and patrons of the sanctuary." That tradition, even in the light of new norms, has always been respected.

Torches and hymns illuminated that procession of faith, which started from Raino and led to Piazza Incoronazione, right there where, 225 years ago, Our Lady was solemnly crowned.

The solemn Eucharistic celebration of the arrival was officiated by Don Antonio De Meo, the general vicar of the diocese of Gaeta; by the clergymen of Itri; and by the rector, Santilli. The homily was directed to Mother Mary's figure as the image of sublime obedience, and to the events concerning the image of the Civita, which through tradition have been sent down for thousands of years. The church of St. Maria Maggiore's *schola cantorum* accompanied, with the ritual hymns, the holy mass; there were moments of deep emotion during the performance of the "Ave Maria," sung by the treble voices choir. At the end of the hymns and invocations for grace, the holy icon was placed on a suitable throne, abundantly adorned, in the church of St. Maria Maggiore. All this happened on July 14.

On the following days, evening encounters were held with mothers, widows, and widowers, and with the elderly and the young. A day dedicated for the sick was held on July 19, visiting them and giving communion to the invalid. Other two days were dedicated to the young who had just been confirmed and to those who had just taken their first communion.

On July 20, the image of the Madonna of the Civita started her journey, in procession, through the streets of *her* Itri, repeated both on the twenty-first and the twenty-second, each with different itineraries.

These are the holy aspects, coordinated by Father Angelo Di Battista, which have distinguished this important appointment of faith for the land of Itri. Thousands of faithful came from many different places. We were stunned by the presence of the many emigrants from the USA, especially from Canada.

The encounter with the Civita was an act of faith for all those who came, knowing that she was momentarily absent. They were convinced that the house of God, the sanctuary, was a place of communion with the supernatural, a meeting of people, and a strengthening of faith—a never-ending pilgrimage that continued even after the celebration rituals.

Thousands of people, just as had happened for the descent, accompanied the return of the holy icon from Itri to the Raino locality. An impressive torch procession and fireworks display could be seen from the sanctuary, greeted good-bye the painting to the Madonna della Civita's staying in Itri. It reached the sanctuary at about eleven, where hundreds of devoted people were awaiting in prayer her arrival. Hundreds of torches illuminated not only faces but every corner of the Square Beato Don Guanella, where the rector, Santilli, and his sanctuary collaborators—along with the faithful followers—attended, reciting the Holy Rosary, and watched from afar the sight of the string of cars that wound up the Valle del Liri.

Father Renato Santilli's homily centered on the Madonna of the Civita's three different tokens of devotion. A speech of particular highlights was that of a police officer from the USA, a message of hope and an appeal, to his own, that the men of this earth should call upon the Virgin of Nazareth's protection, the Lord's humble handmaid of Mother of the Church.

He said, "*The young generation, tomorrow's future, should not only foster the traditions of Itri's land, but they should make their own of the Pope John Paul II's words, which he pronounced on the occasion of the Seventeenth World Youth Day held in Toronto: 'To Mary, Mother of the Church, I entrust each one of you, your vocations and your mission of life.'*" (Pecchia 2003)

In a moment of a well-turned-out celebration, deprived of unruliness, full of meaning and satisfaction, the rector; the mayor, Mr. Giovanni Agresti; and the aldermen, Mr. Vincenzo Ialongo and Mr. Raffaele Mancini, along with other authorities like Mr. Mario Petrillo, president of the committee, appealed to the conscience of those who represented the institution so that youth could find a different reality to that in which they have plunged, a dull modern life without ideals but full of consumerism.

At the end of the mass, the holy icon of the Madonna of the Civita, provided with anti-glare glass for a better visibility, was placed on her throne.

"*Oh, Mary, Mother of Jesus, our Savior, and Mother of the Church*" was Monsignor Farano's prayer, lifted high toward the heavens through the rector Santilli's words, along with the faithful, in a chorus of prayer. It was the conclusion of an event we all experienced with great intensity and religious participation, personally appreciating the entertainment aspect.

At the end of the mass, ritual photos of the civil and religious authorities were taken near the high altar. Felt statements never so convergent as on this occasion were made. All this leaves one's hopes in an always more enthusiastic cooperation on behalf of all, for the good of the faithful and for the growth of the sanctuary.

When everything seemed to suppose (since an hour had passed after midnight) that everyone could go back home, a child's melodious voice, so small that she could not be seen from behind the altar, started singing "*Oh, Mary, from Constantinople*" and immediately, all those present sang along, lifting toward the heavens the most ancient of hymns. In that moment, an ideal baton was being given to the young of this earth, called upon by the adults to hand down in the future, as has happened in the course of these past thousand years, the reverence toward the Virgin Mary that was once called of the Civita (Pecchia 2003).

Chapter 10
Discorso
Don Michele Manzi

Many of us, at one time, read or heard the story of Maria SS della Civita. This *discorso* is a profound history and account, given by the rector of the shrine in 1875 during a trying time in Itri, in which the Itrani population endured much suffering and persecution for their faith. Don Michele Manzi was a well-known orator and a fearless defender of his faith and the rights and faith of the Christian people in Itri and surrounding cities. He was imprisoned with Raffaele Gigante for participation in patriotic activities. Prof. Cav. Antonio Cardi—in a booklet written by him and dedicated to his son, Monsignor Alfredo Cardi of Itri, in 1948, entitled *Tradition and Story of the Maria SS Della Civita, Patron of Itri*—praised Don Michele Manzi. He wrote, "*For seven days orators sang praises to Mary; of the best were Don Michele Manzi from Itri and Canonico Longo from Sessa Aurunca.*" Among the books and the document of the *discorso* my mother Gaetanina gave to me was a command to *scrivi e recorda!* (Write and remember!)

Gaetanina giving information to her daughter Bernadette Conte

The following *discorso* was translated by Robert M. Bucci Jr. The document was an intense work to be translated from Italian into English. Robert spent countless hours and months to give us this account of an historical time for the rector of the Maria SS della Civita Santuario and the Itrani population in Itri, Italy. He did it freely and with all his heart, for the greater glory of our spiritual mother, Mary.

Alla sig.ra Bernadette Conte, USA (sent to me by Pino Pecchia, Italy),

Don Michele Manzi, and the Italian Risorgimento.

Although Itri has been the homeland of Michele Pezza, better known as Fra Diavolo (Frair Devil), who defended the kingdom of Naples because of the Bourbons, the Italian Risorgimento found in the land of Itri a dense band of conspirators who fought for "Unity of Italy."

Among the various characters from Itri that characterized that particular moment in history, was a priest called Father Michele Manzi, friend of important historical figures of the Risorgimento such as Giuseppe Mazzini and Vincenzo Gioberti.

Even if King Ferdinand II knew that he was an ardent member of the Carbonari (secret revolutionary societies with a patriotic and liberal focus), he happily entertained himself playing cards with him when he went to visit the sanctuary of the Madonna della Civita. Don Michael Manzi was the author of an important book that glorified the figure of our Celestial Mother.

The friendship that bound him to King Ferdinand II did not at all condition him. In the square where the first coronation of Her Holy Highness Maria of the Civita took place in 1777, Father Michele Manzi gave a speech against the government of the Bourbons of Naples.

Discourse in honor of Maria Della Civita
Given by the Rector of the Shrine in the Church of the Annunciation (Ave Gratia Plena) in Itri
21 July 1875

Translated by Robert M. Bucci Jr.

Translator's Foreword

"Although delivered 138 years ago to a people who were much different than the people we are today, this sermon nevertheless remains quite relevant to us. By virtue of the gift of hindsight, we can see how the sermon's central message affects anyone who, despite the barriers of time and space, dares to call himself a son of Maria della Civita. After all, it is her feast that most palpably demonstrates the unique bond shared by our actual home of Knightsville with our ancestral home in the town of Itri. That which defines this relationship as *sui generis* is the fact that, despite the immense geographic distance between Knightsville and Itri, the two cities are forever linked by ties at whose core is the desire to preserve a collective identity and tradition—ties between immigrants in the 'new' world and the family and friends that they left behind in the 'old' world.

"The importance of this continuity in tradition—particularly with regard to the filial devotion rendered unto the patroness of Itri, Maria Santissima della Civita—as the pivotal point that links Knightsville to Itri, as the force that enlivens and sustains both communities, cannot be underlined enough. Of course, it is fortuitous that the *itrani* settled in Knightsville, for Knightsville proved to be a place that allowed for them to apply the skills amassed in their homeland to labor opportunities presented in America: a place that allowed them to build the foundation necessary to ensure their capabilities to succeed and prosper. But also of paramount importance to their perseverance was the desire to establish the same sense of community that existed in Itri. It is for this reason that the sustainment of the annual *festa* in honor of the Madonna della Civita so marvelously effectuated the manifestation of a collective solidarity that came to bestow significance and fortitude to the immigrants within the context of their experience in a foreign land.

"Furthermore, the renewal of the feast would prove to provide the common foundation that would join Knightsville to Itri for generations to come. The feast still serves as the reminder that beckons us to look back to our origins: to look back at Itri, to look at that glorious effigy of the Madonna preserved atop Mount Civita, to look back at the miracle procured through her intercession, to look back at her perilous journey to Itri from Constantinople. We must not—we cannot—forget our roots and choose simply to give focus to the traditions that are derived from them, for our origins dictate the course of tradition and determine the organic soundness of tradition's development.[2]

"From Knightsville, on 21 July 2012, the Feast of Maria SS della Civita.
—Robert M. Bucci Jr."

Discourse in Honor of Maria della Civita

NOTICE

The author, well aware of surrounding circumstances, declares that he would have never dared to publish this discourse if it had not disturbed the nerves of some members of municipal representation—the highest in the town[3]—who pointed out to you some offensive propositions, from which have been derived a mark of dissension and the occurrence of my resignation from the office of Rector. I leave it to the intelligent and impartial public to fashion proper judgment in this dispute between the writer and town hall, with the foreword that not a word has been added or subtracted from the originally delivered discourse and that exactly what was recited during the aforementioned religious feast is printed here.

DISCOURSE IN HONOR OF MARIA SS DELLA CIVITA

"*Itrani*, if ever it happened that, among the cheerful circumstances of my appearance on this sacred pulpit, I felt my heart inundate with a torrent of joy, this is precisely the occasion in which, called by you, I come down from the mountain of wonders, a messenger and exhibitor of the most prodigious event that is a unique and immortal glory of our land and a well felt pride. And since the commemoration of the divine event is always new, always beautiful, you continually listen; you marvel. He who at the dawn of time extracted the universe from the dark abyss, in whose presence a difference of persons or things is not illustrated, to whose thought the worn cloak of the poor man and the crimson adornments of kings have the same origin, the same fate; He whose power is equal to will, even though He inhabits inaccessible light, still from there, completely moving His glory through the universe, permeates and shines forth—His infinite majesty fills the heavens, the earth, and abysses. Thus all creation directs its intellectual gaze to the presence of God, each creature naturally means to recognize its maker, and even the littlest bird and the smallest flower in their semblance affirm: 'We are because God made us.' Therefore, each space of creation is an altar, and nature a temple, that God fills with His grandeur. In the reflection of this divine light, which bounces off the infinite series of existents, man, with a leap of love and veneration, transports his soul into the womb of divinity, from that inexhaustible source of the courage that is necessary in the trials of life, from that inexhaustible source of the nobility of thoughts and the purity of emotions which, detaching man from earthly life, turn mortal man himself toward the blessed dwellings of eternity. Wherever urged by religious sentiment, the poor descendant of Adam can open his heart to joy—wherever a sigh reaches the womb of God, wherever one can gather under the wings of providence; in meditation, in prayer, man can taste a joy heralding the rejoicing of paradise. Only the wicked man trembles everywhere, because in this immense shrine of creation he alone is profane. But if the majesty of God fills the universe, and each creature with its natural language deduces His existence and propagates His glory, it is similarly most true that the Eternal Maker, in order to make man hear His enthralling and mysterious voice, wants man to sequester himself from crowds and from public shouting in order to ascend the mountain and enter into solitude, into silence, the due sacrifice of the mind and heart. Abraham ascends the mountain to sacrifice Isaac and sees God; the mountain is where Moses receives God's Law; the mountain is where Elijah speaks with God; our Redeemer Himself ascends the mountain; Mary passes through the mountains of Judah and carries herself to the priestly city of Hebron[1]—Mary in the city of Hebron![4] And here, good people, I cannot contain my joy and hold back my happiness for the grateful

---

[1] Hebron is a city south of Jerusalem. It was the home of Elizabeth and Zacharias, the parents of John the Baptist. It was there that Mary visited her cousin Elizabeth.

memory of the journey of mother of God through the mountains—the joy that I read in your expressions, gushing forth in sweet smile, is already a foreboding of my own thought—she who, in joining into similar marvelous events, flew from the mountains of Judah to the new city of God. The new city of God! Yes, and I, with you all—proud of the name *Itrano*, the name of a people more fortunate than the inhabitants of the city of Levi—participate with all reason in the exultation of possessing in one of our mountains heaven's enviable entrustment of her in whom God Himself prepared His celestial sojourn. Yes, Mary, the august temple of God, the domicile of heaven and earth, the ire, the blindness, fleeing from that people that still the Sultan corrects, chose Mount Civita as her dwelling, just as long ago the Ark of the Lord, fleeing the cruel Philistines, chose Abinadab[2] and Zion. Mount Civita . . . Ah, be silent, Hebrew nation; if the omnipotent right hand visibly worked unprecedented wonders on you in the Red Sea, and then at Sinai, and all the way to the Promised Land of Canaan, we too—without envying your fortune—chosen by the highest, inscrutable designs for a the promised land of heaven, possess its unmistaken token in the blessed Tabor[3] of Mount Civita. There, oh mercy, the tabernacle placed between heaven and earth, infinite majesty almost confined, puts Mount Civita in communication with the throne of God. Oh wonder! Oh enviable boast! Oh glory! *Itrani*, my fellow citizens, the dawn of this day has been and will always be sacred for us, solemn for us; and I, on the occasion of the anniversary of this religious feast consecrated to the outlet of joy, of happiness, I, whose age turning to evening is averse to the smooth orators and the inauthentic beggar, I have but one thing to say: Itri, chosen by God to possess in Mount Civita the miraculous portrait of Mary of Constantinople, this, yes, this is your only true glory. *Gloria Domini super te est*—the glory of the Lord is upon you. Therefore, Mount Civita, where God pours out the fullness of His glory upon the image of Mary, is the mountain of wonders, the mountain of peace, the pledge of future glory. In a word, our glory is to possess a land that communicates with heaven. *Itrani*, I consider it superfluous, rather offensive, to commend me to you benevolence. An *itrano* who speaks of the glory of Itri is by himself commended.

Before the insufficient ship of my mind deploys its torn sails[4] from the Byzantine strait to follow the marvelous happening all the way to Mount Civita, that event which today makes us all happy and proud, it is necessary, good people, that I worry your attention against the vexatious insinuation of some innovative spirits, who, either because of excessive reasoning, wander in the hypothetical and unknown, or, as

---

[2] Abinadab was a Levite in whose house the Ark of the Covenant was kept after being brought back from the land of the Philistines. Twenty years later, David moved it to Mount Zion.

[3] Mount Tabor is a mountain in the Jezreel Valley in Lower Galilee where the Transfiguration of the Lord occurred.

[4] The author here alludes to the initial verses of canto I of Dante Alighieri's *Purgatorio*.

packs concentrated on search of sensible things that have lost wellness of mind, qualify outward worship of the Divine as injurious and pass off the use and veneration of sacred images as idolatry or, at least, superstitious.[5] But if these novel iconoclasts consider for a short while their belonging to the human species, would they not bump into the rocks of strangeness, of impiety? Since man is so made by nature to need sensible excitement for the apprehension of truth and the adhesion to the good, one cannot hence be removed from imaginative signs and symbols in the successive unfolding of truth and desire to be continually excited from fire of the objects of one's affection in the carrying out of one's own duties. For that, outward worship, although it does not constitute the essence of religion, is nonetheless the necessary means to vivify and fortify religious sentiment and to promote moral and civil improvement.

"The aspect of the temple of God with venerable rites and sacrifices, the celestial word of the sacred minister who in the name of God calls for respect for leaders and observance of laws; the wonders of painting and sculpture, symbols relative to the original; vocal harmonies and sounds all bring impressions of sensible truth, and, almost divinizing the spirit, elevate it to where the Divine Essence shines. But how? Is it perhaps licit to honor through statues and images the memory of renowned men for their civic virtues and military triumphs, and then deem worship and the veneration of sacred images as idolatry or superstition? It is in such contractions that the enemies of religion and disturbers of social order wrap themselves. And as there is no society without duties—nor duties without laws, nor laws without legislators, nor legislators without God, from whom constituted authority emanates—so for these humanitarians of the school of de La Mettrie, and of oil, for these humanitarians who have eliminated religion, force would be without control, without reason, without advice; men would be without laws, vice without blame, virtue without praise; society would be an anarchy, a chaos whose supreme law would be brute force, egoism, terrorism. Strange dreams of the infirm mind. Full of misfortune, we were reserved, good people, to times so light and superficial, that, scorning all ancient wisdom with stunning haughtiness and trampling upon history and the experience of all past generations, we deigned this first daughter of heaven a mere nothing, an old family tool now useless, or rather an encumbrance, a hindrance to glory and to prosperity, to the progress of nations, so much as to even ask for entire separation from her. Do they not know that religious sentiment forms the whole horizon of humanity? Only it opens the perspective of the infinite to society and, equally, to each individual. This sentiment is the only one that lifts the people up from miseries, that raises the happy folk of the time above their egoism, as Lamartine says.[6]

---

[5]   The Xenophon (c. 430-354 BC) was a Greek historian, soldier, and philosopher who was one of the first thinkers to argue that the cosmos had to have been conceived by a god or gods.

"The most religious nations, states Xenophon,⁵ were also the wisest, and they prospered longer. Each social law must be to you like a voice that descends from heaven—a phrase of the most moral Seneca.⁶ The cry of war of those peoples was *pugnamus pro aris, et focis*—for God and country, for altars and for hearths; the altar, and the domestic roof, one's name, and the fatherland were all one. But I do not want to ravage the joy of this day with bitter considerations; and since the impious follies of the new iconoclasts took me far from my principal intention, I return now to my intended proposition. But if there be among you, good people, someone who in the movements of the procession stops me, asking me desirously why God in this, more than in any other image of Mary, desired to pour the full extent of his glory in order that it be a mystery of divine plans into which man is not allowed penetrate, I respond instead that in me a thought is stirred that dates back to the eighth century, and which signals to me, if I think correctly, the exposition of the miracle, where history and fact demonstrate with evidence the Most High to have deigned the people of Itri to possess on Mount Civita this glorious image of Mary. And truth be told, with the darkness of night having fled, thanks to the evangelical light from that region where the Danube finds course, and that the Black Sea and the Sea of Marmara bathe, in ancient Byzantium, now the city of Constantine, a sun shone blazingly as if in its midday position—that is, the religion of Christ—when, in the year 726 of the common era, heaven became cloudy, the day became dark, and a shaking whirlwind of persecution exploded. The light of the temple was extinguished, and sacred images were extirpated from domestic lairs, torn apart, and incinerated. The iconoclast persecution begun and urged by the wrathful order of Emperor Leo III the Isaurian, roaring as does the sea during a storm, made its horrible and desolate echo heard even as far as Italy. But the marvelous image of Mary of Constantinople was untouched by the frantic whirlwind.

"Afterwards, in the midst of the rage of the infernal storm, two men, Basilian monks from the shrine erected in honor of Mary by the heroine St. Pulcheria, removed the precious portrait, hid it in a crate, and anxiously took it to those portions of the land that bend around the marina. Discovered and reached by some soldiers who were desirous of only gold and silver, the sacred deposit was stopped, rummaged through, and, among these soldiers' imagined false hopes, yet another false hope was wickedly enclosed with the painting and the two blessed keepers and thrown to the mercy of the sea. No sooner said than done.

"Already I hear its splash—and the sultry mood welcomes it desirously; pushed onward by one smiling wave after another to the slopes of Cilicia, this ark of the Lord, not in the least way reluctant, kissed the shore. Thereupon, amidst the stupor and wonder—seeing that the two blessed monks were still alive—the image was

---

6   Seneca (4 BC-AD 65) was a Roman statesman, dramatist, and philosopher who was the tutor and advisor of the emperor Nero.

taken with triumphant religious pomp into the most important church of Ithaca.[7] But the marvelous occurrence does not stop here, for He who can do that which He wills reserved in His inscrutable plans so much glory for Itri. And truth be told, with Cilicia invaded by the barbaric Muslim hordes, the sacred image vanished and made a stop and took rest on coast of Messina. Attentive in midst of the joy, that people welcomed the wonder and placed the celestial treasure in the temple of the Lord. But this was transient—their fortune was of short duration—for the Most High had designated to place on the soil of Itri the mystical tabernacle in which He communicated the extent of His glory. Not so candid a cloud, hovering over the sea by ethereal means, hardly presented itself into view, like Mary on the Sicilian shore; almost as if beating its wings up to an oak tree on Mount Civita, the prodigious flight stopped there, but the miracle does not. An ox, unmindful of food, abandons its herd and prostrates itself reverently at the foot of the oak tree. With the ox finally discovered by the attentive and worried peasant, he now finds himself before a vivid light emanating from the tree—just as brilliant as the bush on Mount Horeb[7]; uncertain at first if he is the spectator of a ghost or reality, but then having succumbed to adoration, he propagates before day's end the marvelous occurrence. And here, good people, since my tongue is unable to express just how much the throng of my simultaneous and various thoughts suggests, I leave it to your imagination to conceive the exuberance of joy, of jubilee, when all persons without distinction of sex, age, or condition, left their respective abodes for this happy and unexpected arrival, went to the new Horeb, and, overwhelmed and taken by religious stupor, remained in the sight of this new marvel. But not even here does this wonder end. While the exultant religious procession proceeded toward Itri and the valley resounded with hymns and spiritual songs—interrupted only by cries of compassion and sighs of consolation in the sight of these new unprecedented wonders—the house of divine Wisdom came here, the temple of the glory of the Lord with solemn rite was placed here in this church dedicated to the Seraphic Father of Mount Alvernia, St. Francis. But who could laugh at the throbbing of hearts, the anguish, the surprise in seeing the sacred image disappear from behind locked doors and flee back to the mountain to rest exactly there where it had been? The thought arose then, naturally and unanimously, that the Most High had arranged, like at other times, that the wonders of His glory would be made manifest on mountains, and that He had destined the mountain where she still is as the resting place of the glorious Queen of the universe and this city of His vision of peace as immortal. Great God, yes, to You always all laud and glory! *Magnus Dominus et laudabilis nimis*—great Lord, praised magnanimously—who in glorifying Mary on our holy mountain, You made us glorious among our equals, and proud *in civitate Dei nostri, in monte sancto ejus*[8]—in the city of our God, on His holy mountain. But

---

[7] Mount Horeb is the mountain where Moses encountered the burning bush.

the Most High is not yet contented to exalt her, if it truly was she who returned from Lebanon with her forehead not encompassed by a golden crown.

"Already the sun of July completes its ninety-eighth orbit since the prelates of Mount Horeb[7] is the mountain where Moses encountered the burning bush.

"Sessa, Gaeta, and Fondi convened on this same day, in this same renowned town, to crown our glorious Lady.[8] And the solemn religious pomp was mixed in marvels, as was the display of apparatus in midst of the joyous fluttering of so many people, such that I would dare to say that an echo was made then, and, even so astonishing, it did not stop in the middle of its course through the vague hills and nearby mountains—at least until, despite heaven, the great star of nature turned to its setting.

"*Itrani*, the mystical tower of David in communication with the throne of God, surmounted by a crown of gold, but with more happy patronage, is already placed on Mount Civita, and I can affirm without fear of error that never was the glory of the Lord shown so evidently as in this miraculous happening. I know that the ark of the ancient covenant was a vagabond and that Shiloh, Cariaterim, and Gilead, and Nob saw it wandering—not on leveled wings, but rather on the arms of the Levites—and sometimes willfully left with untamed heifers, or even propped up either by a rod or by the menacing shout the herdsman soldier. The first ark was left in the palace of David and then in most renown Temple, many times surrendered to hardships, and then in open field among the harvesting scythes, and then under the private roofs of Abinadab and of Obededon; but the prodigious ark of the covenant with Itri glided quite lightly on the summit of the waves and recognized no other resting place than the temple outside of and in the homeland of Odysseus, and then in the whirlpool of Charybdis in Messina;[9] finally, taken gloriously on the feathers of the winds, it now rests on the Mount Tabor of Itri, Mount Civita: *Gloriosa dicta sunt de te, civitas Dei*[10]—glorious things are said of you, city of God! Itri, envied possessor of so much glory, forget in this moment any another honor if you even have any, and rise above yourself justly proud. For you, and you know it well, nothing else remains in that rocky chain of alpine and nude mountains besides that mountain where the bulwark of Zion lays, in which is contained the ark of the Lord, your only and sole glory—the marvelous ark, respected and safe from common wreckage. You are the true testimony, the industrious instrument, the bright theater of the glory of Maria della Civita. Come now! Raise your heads, turn your eyes, and with anxious confusion gaze at how the attendance of devotees fills you, how it floods you. From surrounding and more far-off regions, there is not a province, a city, a neighborhood, or a village that, with fatherland and family abandoned, does not embark upon the comfortless

---

[8] Psalm 48:2.

[9] Charybdis is, in Greek mythology, a monstrous whirlpool located in the Strait of Messina.

[10] Psalm 87:3.

journey with religious silence and fervid prayer. Similar to the leader of Israel who, taken by veneration and holy fear, goes silently forward with bare feet to Mount Horeb in order to hear the voice of God, the devote pilgrim of Mary, in ascending the Mount Horeb of Itri with shoes taken off, hair untied, with a heart trembling in tenderness and joy at the sight of the glorious tabernacle of the Lord, makes the solitary valley resound with cries and shrieks, which sometimes graze our faces with the dust of their call. You saw still important princes, most eminent cardinals, distinct prelates, Supreme Pontiffs—among Charybdis[9] is, in Greek mythology, a monstrous whirlpool located in the Strait of Messina.[1]

These, the current Pope, the great Pius IX[9]—the magnanimous King Ferdinand with the royal family, who, in the inauspicious days of his reign, leveled the steep slopes of the mountain with a carriageway.

"But do not stop just yet, stretch your vision even further and you will see the devotion of your venerable Lady extend in a wondrous way; better yet, it has arrived at such a point that there is no apartment building, house, dwelling, or slum that does not maintain devotion to her for protection, for infallible garrison. *Leva oculos tuos, et vide*[11]—raise your eyes and see! You will see . . . but who could ever trace the rapid progress of so marvelous a devotion? That small source, which, breaking into a scant stream, murmurs between stone and stone, and slowly twists through the steep valley, leaving behind grassy strips with vague flowers, welcomes creeks on the way, and grows into brooks in such a way that, widening the banks, a swollen river arrives at and bumps into, and presses, and shakes, and passes, and floods all surrounding lands with its overwhelming bed; analogously, good people, in the miraculous veneration of Mary the dream of Mordecai[12] has come true: *Parvus fons crevit in fluvium*[13]—the little fountain grew into the river. And after such and so many marvelous occurrences, who could doubt for an instant that Itri has not been chosen by God for the pride of possessing on Mount Civita the wonderful image of Mary? Therefore, Mount Civita is not only the mount of wonders; it is the true and only pride of Itri, but, at the same time, the pledge of future glory, the pledge that communicates with heaven, or, rather, with the throne of God.

The existence of future life is a truth recognized by all peoples of every religion, the new idolaters not excluded. After all, if it did not exist, it would not be an object of thought, nor the end to which will irresistibly tends, because to think and want nothing is an absurdity, and God is infallible. And truth be told, good people, our existence is not a single point in the immense circle of time, and it can be called, along with the prophet, 'the fragile vessel' that goes sailing the

---

[11] Isaiah 49:18.

[12] Mordecai was the cousin of Esther and one of the main personages in the book of Esther. He had a dream in which he saw a little fountain flow and grow into a river.

[13] Esther 10:6.

ocean of eternity. Since there is no properly defined end to human life, but only a period of existence, then another period succeeds it; so it is not absurd to say that our earthly days are enclosed by two births, one of which transmits us to the earth, the other of which transports us into heaven. If our destiny was that of being born similarly to the beasts of the forest, of living and lacking amid sensations of pleasure and sadness in order to afterwards only return to become one with the soil of the earth, for what end would the Creator have enriched the soul with so many faculties, the complete development of which requires nothing less than eternity? If the horizon of earth has not intersected with that of heaven, and if the human soul—this spark of the eternal flame of divine light—must pass away in the stone of a tomb, God would not have imprinted in the soul the desire for happiness and for eternal life. But to achieve such happiness is naturally impossible in this earthly life, where goods end because they are exhaustible and it is instead vane to appease the innate tendencies that overwhelm the heart with misery, nuisance, and anguish; it is therefore necessary to elevate oneself above the sphere of sensibility and offer God the continuous sacrifice of body to spirit, of sense to reason, of appetite to conscience in order to enjoy peace, the yearned for calm of heart, where is hidden that ray of relative happiness that comes forth from the absolute Good.[10]

"And as psychological law explains the activity of the spirit in broad dimensions as being increasingly sequestered by an indefinite serious of existents that destroy the spirit with their impressions in a diverse way—with solitude—silence remains the place where God speaks to man, where He shows Himself to man, and where he infuses into the soul of man a torrent of pleasure without end. But where God manifests Himself to creation, in that place is there not peace and true happiness? Therefore, solitude is the place where the soul finds in silence the peace of passions and foretastes the ineffable sweetness of future glory in as much as is allowable to the human condition. And if the patriarch Jacob burst forth awake and ecstatic from his vision, 'Here is the house of God and the gate of heaven,' then I can probably speak of Mount Civita, good people, as the place where divine wisdom has placed its royal habitation in the illustrious mother of God made man. *Sapientia aedificavit sibi domum*[14]—wisdom has built a house for itself—as said by the abbot of Chiaravalle: the house of God's delights. I will say that on that blessed mountain we have the mystical city illuminated by heaven, because there burns that candelabrum to which the spark of the eternal Sun sets fire, *e coelo accipiens ignem*—and heaven is accepting of the fire. I will say that on Mount Civita, the true city of God gives us a foretaste of itself and prepares us for the beatific vision; *parat nobis Dei visum*—it prepares the vision of God for us. I will say that Mount Civita is the heaven of the soul, that there is found full peace and content, because, with Mary being there, entrance is prohibited to

---

[14] Proverbs 9:1.

the enemy of every good. I will say that Mount Civita is the inexhaustible source of that happiness which is promised to us, of that tranquility that surpasses each sentiment, of that joy that captivates us, because there in the womb of Mary rests the paradise of all pleasantry and therefore the worth of future glory. I will say that from Mount Civita flows forth that unfailing river of grace, which, flowing with impetus, beautifies and cheers that city of God. I will say finally that on Mount Civita is placed that glorious ark of the covenant with Itri, where that mysterious stair whose summit rests on the throne of God reposes, puts the earthly Jerusalem in communication with the celestial Jerusalem. In a word, while Mount Civita constitutes the true and sole glory of Itri—the mountain of wonders—it is also the mountain of peace, where the devoted soul finds the gate of happiness between earthly and celestial paradise in the stormy ocean of the world. But if someone wanted to deem my reasoning as strange, as exaggerated, let him climb the Tabor of Itri and he will find what I say to be nothing less than true. He will see, especially when heaven extraordinarily beckons to the singing of humble prayer, an invisible force take him away from the life of the senses and spread itself like a pure cloud—admirable effect of the majesty of God—and come to permeate the temple. Yes, it is then that heart of the true believer and devotee of Mary, touched by a mysterious superhuman language, is elevated from the impressions of ordinary life and swims in an unbounded sea of peace, of happiness.

"He lives, but he does not know anything of living."[11] Those suave enticements of language without words in turn arouse joy, meditation, transposition; and evoking melancholy from the darkest glooms of the past, the most soave memories take thought to the regions of a future and incomprehensible world: they put it into a state akin to paradise, they make it extremely happy. He lives, and yet he knows nothing of living. The seductive and varied worldly scenes now in oblivion are finished; no longer do love, hatred, fear, hope, anguish, and anxiety render living miserable. He lives but knows nothing of living, because he already stands there where the eye of the just man discovers a new horizon and how, like a dream in the night, the illusions of earth fade away. He lives but knows nothing of living, because everything smiles for him and heaven is dominated by the new and always growing desire to hover on the wings of love in order to taste once again the celestial sweetness of peace of heart. Just as the quick swallow ranges over the plain and river, arrives at swashing the water, rises, goes back up into the air hovering on its tireless feathers, turns, and then chirps in heaven, so does the devout soul still fix its gaze upon the glorious Queen of the universe, the mystical Zion of peace, that throne of the glory of God, that depository and arbiter of divine treasures. Yes, my fellow citizens, this is the continued miracle that is fulfilled on the holy mount. But what can be said then of the marvels varied in kind and in resounding quality, of which we and the visitors of the city of God—visitors from near and far—cannot help but admire and celebrate the beneficence and glory? Through her, the crippled are healed, the languid strengthened; through her, speech is restored to the mute, hearing to the death, and the use of the limbs to the paralyzed. Through her, thunderbolts are stifled in the air, the shipwrecked are saved, swords are broken, and the decrepit are held up. But I do not intend to review these and the other private graces bestowed because, when the sun later begins to set, such a recount would only have reached its climax. The very many favors and votives that honor and adorn these sacred walls speak for themselves! Speak of her, good people!

"May your children speak of her! And later on may your grandchildren speak of her! May they raise from our honored tombs the cape venerating our praises and speak of her! They'll remember us among the continuous serious of so many marvels: the cessation of the plague, the multiplication of bread, the defeat of bandits. Still, even we remember the various massacres of the tragic Asian disease from which we have always been immune. We even remember the imminent disasters and perils that our homeland evaded only because our most affectionate Mother stretched her glorious embrace upon us. We remember finally—but remember more, we could—if the prodigious occurrence fulfilling itself on Mount Civita shows with force that God destined Itri to glory of holding the miraculous portrait of Mary of Constantinople, and, for that, if Mount Civita is the mountain of wonders, the place of peace, the place where earth communicates with heaven, the true and sole glory Itri will endure as long as the world is not dissolved. But so much glory and, justifiably, so much pride would not have any reason—better yet, another reason would not be needed—than to fill us with shame and turmoil if we were to be present at the pitiful spectacle of seeing devout pilgrims fall into tears in the midst of fervent prayers and, with barefoot feet and vivid faith, ascend the mount of wonder only out of desire to gaze upon Mary, while we instead were occupied in profane conversations,[12] sometimes licentious, perhaps even until a wise connoisseur seized the thought of them.

"Away then from the holy mountain, you unbeliever, you ill-doer, you who are interested solely in the which is worldly, you immodest ones—do not even dare to place your profane foot down in this place; *foris canes, foris adulteri*—away you dogs, you adulterers! Away you murderers, you liars, you vile evil speakers, you despicable slanderers! *Foris homicida, et qui amat, et facit mendacium*[15]—away you who murder, you who claim to love and make lies—and let him be removed from his place as a citizen of Itri, he who would attend to scandals of this nature, and, only after, would seem to promote and love ardently the glory of Mary. No, certainly, he is not *Itrano*; those who are desecrators of this sacred space, those who are hospitable to him for his service in municipal affairs, solely to serve their own ambitious ends and private interests, these men are cursed! One should be consumed completely in thought, will, and action to promote the glory of Mary,

---

[15] Revelation 22:15.

who is truly ours and our sole glory, in order to be deigned worthy of preceding the ark of manna come down from the realm of the clouds. This is why today, reminded by religious pomp and joy, we renew the faith that our hearts overflow with and we imitate the fervor of your ancestors. We affirm the sincere resolution and issue the same oath to forget past failures and to promote the veneration and devotion of Mary always more and more in the days and years to come, and we do so in order that the present age announce to the successive age—father to son, and later on the son to his children, all the way through the generations of man— that God chose the people of Itri to possess glory on Mount Civita—the mountain of peace, the sister-land of heaven—the glorious image of Mary of Constantinople, the true and sole pride of Itri. *Gloria Domini super te orta est*[16]—the glory of the Lord is risen upon you!

"Closing this solemn and memory-filled day with a regard of obliged gratitude to her, whom the Most High destined to our glory and sole favor, onward comes then the end of so much exuberance. Everyone, lift your heads toward the Zion of Itri; keeping your gazes fixed with mine, imitate the son of Isaiah, and burst forth in loving song!

"Oh beautiful city of Zion, yours are the foundations on the holy mountain of God, who loves your gates more than any other house of Jacob! Great and marvelous things are said of you, and will be said of you, oh city descended from heaven! Here the farthest-off pilgrims from Tyre and Ethiopia—saints and sinners—flow into your womb. Who will ever say that Zion is the work of human hands, the dwelling place of men, the foundation of the Most High? Yes, when nothing else of your ineffable grandeur is known, let this be recalled: that God Himself was your founder, beautiful city; this, oh beautiful city, is the highest of every praise.[13]

"*Ipse fundavit eam Altissimus*[17]—the Most High Himself has founded her.

"Hail, therefore, Zion of Itri, oh sister-land of heaven, oh Eden of peace; fill the hearts of all those who are consumed by you with your peace. You see always bloom in your womb the cedar of Lebanon, the cypress of Zion, the palm of Kedesh, the rose of Jericho, the olive of peace; you, the iris that surrounds the throne of God, let that our will—we, your honored sons—be open always to better counsel.

"Hail, oh glorious Mother of God made man; as long as the bright stars navigate the ocean of immense space with their orbit, we, the most recent descendents of our forefathers, will sing your praises, will love your honor most ardently, will carry on proudly in your service under the shield of your almighty support, arbiter of the wants of God.

---

[16] Isaiah 60:1.
[17] Psalm 87:5.

"Hail, oh glorious Mother of God made man, daughter of your Son; you are she who ennobled human nature so that the Creator of man did not disdain to make Himself in you.[18] If in heaven you shine with love as the midday torch, and down here among morals you are the living fountain hope, we, chosen by God for this fount of endless graces, have its true source in you on this blessed mountain. And because you are so great, and value so much that your kindness cannot help but assist he who begs your assistance—and how many asking breaths do you anticipate—listen this morning to the supplication and humble prayer of your afflicted children, sighing in harsh exile. Disperse and dispel into the deserts of Cirone the dark whirlwind that bellows and shakes and fixes lies at the foot of the true Eternal One. Always keep your heart vigilant over ours, and, when we are taken in dubious harm and the enemy of everything good inclines us to peril, oh free us from his dreadful treachery. And when our life turns toward its twilight, then in that unknown hour more than ever, assist us so that we, faithful to your patronage and keeping our pupils impatiently fixed on that glorious mountain—hovering on the wings of love—will enter jubilantly into the house of the Lord where the sun neither rises nor sets, singing in union with the royal prophet: *Laetatus sum in his quae dicta sunt mihi; in domum Domini ibimus*[19]—I rejoiced at the things that were said to me; we shall go into the house of the Lord."

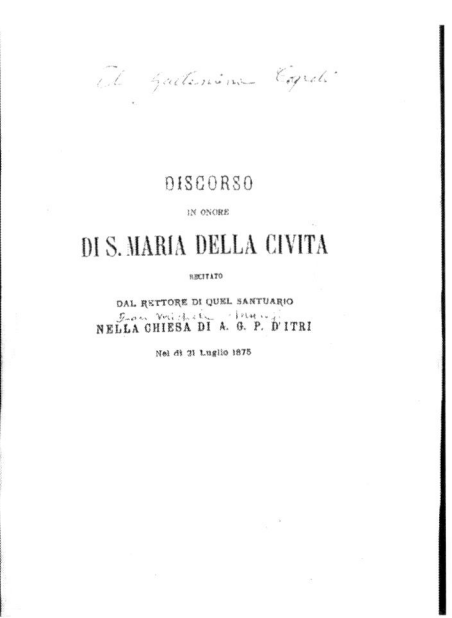

---

[18] The author here alludes to the initial verses of canto XXXIII of Dante's *Paradiso*.
[19] Psalm 122: 1.

CHAPTER 11

Our Beginnings

Initially, the Italian community attended worship at St. Ann's Church on Cranston Street. Some went as far as St. Rocco's Church in Johnston to listen to services in their own language. As time went along and their numbers grew, the people longed for a church of their own. Many could not read or write, and it became difficult to communicate with those who spoke fluent English. They experienced much ridicule by other nationalities, and hostilities mounted. By 1921, the Italian population of the area numbered more than 3,500 people in nearly four hundred families.

The needed sixty dollars was collected from the Itrani community to purchase a statue of their patron saint. The statue had been commissioned and purchased by contributions of the Itrani community. Representing the community, Michele Saccoccia and his sons, Angelo and Nicola, were responsible for the communication and ordering of the statue, with A. Da Prato & Co., from Boston, Massachusetts, who made fine church statuary.

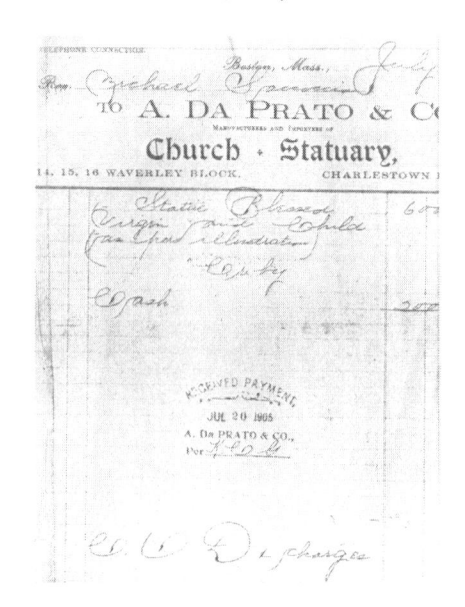

> A. DA PRATO & CO.
> MAKERS OF
> **Fine Church Statuary**
> SCULPTORS, DESIGNERS AND DECORATORS
> 14, 15, 16 Waverley Block   Charlestown District
> BOSTON, MASS.
>
> July 18, 1905.
>
> Mr. Michael Saccoccia,
>   Cranston, (Providence)
>   Rhode Island.
>
> My dear Sir:—
>
> We have your statue almost completed and will ship the same to you on Friday morning next by express, so that you will get it the same evening.
>
> Hoping that this will be satisfactory to you, we remain,
>
> Yours very respectfully,
>
> A. Da Prato & Co.

Bill of Sale and receipt of payment (R, Anderson)

The statue of Maria SS della Civita was delivered July 18, 1905.

Original statue of Maria SS. della Civita

The Itrani community did not spare anything to celebrate their feast. The new and first statue of the Madonna was in a nave above the main altar, in the old St. Rocco's Church.

Original statue above the altar at old St. Rocco's Church
(Rev. Angelo Carusi)

Itrani community with original statue, day of the feast at old St. Rocco's Church

Procession with original statue

Men from the community walked to St. Rocco's Church and returned to Knightsville carrying their Madonna on their shoulders to prepare for the novena and celebration in honor of their patron saint. The novena to Maria SS della Civita was usually held at a home on C Street, according to the elders I interviewed.

On July 21, 1919, the streets in the neighborhood of the city hall corner were festooned with colored lights, and there were many decorations about the streets. Stands for the sale of Italian delicacies were erected and had done a good business. The evening before, a crowd of several hundred gathered to listen to a band concert that was given by the Capone's Band. Selections from an opera were played. The merrymaking was the first since beginning of the war and was, therefore, in the nature of a jubilation over the close of hostilities not one for this country but for Italy. (*Evening Bulletin* 1919)

Celebration at Eugene Perry Square—WW1 (Cranston Historical Society)

Cranston's largest group of drafties in 1917, on their way to
Camp Meade, MD. (Cranston Historical Society)

There was a church parade that day with services at St. Rocco's Church, Thornton, and that evening there was another band concert and a display of fireworks.

Fr. Schettini addresses the crowd gathered to celebrate the 150th anniversary of the Coronation of Maria SS della Civita on the site of the proposed St. Mary's Church, on Haven Avenue and Cranston St. 1927.

Second statue entering the procession

To celebrate the coronation, on July 20, 1927, a two-day festival to celebrate the 150th anniversary of the coronation of the Maria SS della Civita started that day and lasted over until the next evening. The entire Italian population of Knightsville took part in this celebration. The streets through which the procession passed were decorated by stringing many colored electric bulbs across the streets at numerous intervals. The affair cost over $2,100 and was the most impressive and picturesque religious ceremony ever attempted in this city.

The festivities commenced at seven o'clock, with a salute of aerial bombs, set off by Clem Soscia, whose father, John, had previously set up three pinwheels for the first American version of the feast.

Clem Soscia (Providence Journal)

The bombs were to announce that the civic and religious ceremonies in honor of the Blessed Mother were under way. This was followed by a parade through the principal streets of the Italian colony under the numerous colored lights (*Providence Journal* 1953).

The Colonial Band and D'Orsi Silver Lake Band furnished music for the march and also presented a concert at the field behind the city hall on Phenix Avenue.

On Thursday morning at seven thirty, a salute of twenty-one bombs was given, and the band led a procession to St. Mary's Church, formerly St. Ann's, on Church Street, where a high mass was to be held. After this service, the new figure of the Madonna della Civita was carried from the church to the parish grounds where it received a specially made gold crown crafted by Nicola Saccoccia, son of Michele, a skilled jewelry toolmaker.

Michele Saccoccia (Rita S. Anderson)

Nicola Saccoccia (Rita S. Anderson)

The procession then started from the church and marched through the principal Italian streets, with a few selected people who bid as high as $100 for the right to carry the figure of the Madonna.

1st crown make by Nicola Saccoccia (Rita S. Anderson)

Some of the faithful worshipers followed the image along the hot pavement barefoot to do penance.

Itrani women marching

The program on Thursday evening consisted of a band concert at the lot back of the city hall from five thirty to six thirty o'clock and later from eight to ten thirty. At eleven, there was a display of fireworks at the Garden Plat off Cranston Street below the city hall, and this important celebration was concluded (*Cranston News*, July 20, 1927).

Chapter 12
Shepherd My People

Much frustration and anger mounted in the community. The Itrani people needed their own church; they were tired of the persecution their families were enduring.

Antonio B. Cardi, founder, and first trustee of St. Mary's Church

One of Antonio B. Cardi's daughter's came home crying after having gone to confession at St. Ann's Church. She had been harassed and verbally abused. When Antonio heard what had happened to his daughter, he became enraged. He vowed, "Enough—we've had enough. We are going to have our own church." To initiate his plan, he went to the home of his wife Maria Civita Saccoccio's cousin, Luigi Merluzzo, and asked him to join in his efforts.

Luigi Merluzzo, founder

Together, they told the community of their plans. In 1921, the men formed a group called the Italian committee.

Luigi Vallone, founder and first trustee of St. Mary's Church

They solicited help from Luigi Vallone, who became a powerful spokesperson and advocate for the Italian committee and played a major role in the development of St. Mary's Church

Committees were formed, and they worked tirelessly to achieve its objectives by means of a series of open letters to the bishop and personal meetings with various church officials. By January 1922, their efforts were partially rewarded. Bishop William Hickey believed that the Italian population in Cranston needed to be ministered to by a priest who spoke their own language. On January 22, he assigned Reverend Cesare Schettini as an assistant to St. Ann's Church.

Reverend Cesare Schettini, first Pastor and founder of St. Mary's Church

Father Schettini was born on August 15, 1884, in Vicovaro, Rome. After attending public schools in Vicovaro, he went to college at Tivoli and continued his studies for the priesthood there. Bishop Scaccia ordained him on June 18, 1905, at the young age of twenty. His "early" ordination required a papal dispensation. After one year of further study, he was appointed a professor at Tivoli Seminary. He served briefly there until 1908 when he was appointed pastor of Our Lady of Victories Church, Tivoli. During his pastorate, he gained diocesan recognition while serving as a member of the Mission Band, a group of clergy who devoted their energies toward conversion. With the coming of World War I, Father Schettini volunteered for duty as a chaplain in the Italian army.

Following the Versailles Treaty, Father Schettini applied for missionary work with the Italians in America. Initially, he served at St. Joachim's Parish in New York City, but at the end of 1919, he came to Rhode Island and was assigned as an assistant to Reverend Antonio Bove at St. Ann's Church, Providence. After conversing with Father Bove, Bishop Hickey decided to send Father Schettini to Cranston.

The young priest began his ministry to the people of Knightsville by celebrating two masses each week in the basement of St. Ann's. He met and began to work with the Italian committee to achieve its long-sought goal for an Italian parish in Cranston. The committee was disheartened because the Italian population had grown so much that it far surpassed the entire parish family of St. Ann's, yet the bishop moved cautiously. Letters to him went unanswered, and requests for subsequent interviews were denied.

The Italian community and Father Schettini's every move was reported to the bishop by Reverend Thomas Tiernan, pastor of St. Ann's Church. Father Tiernan wrote letters to the bishop reporting every activity of the Itrani community. The Italian community advertised for a fund-raising event they had planned. Their goal was to raise money for the specific purpose of purchasing land for their future church and their building fund. In a letter written to Bishop William Hickey, Father Tiernan reported the following message:

> The following notice was posted on a large signboard [6 × 4] at eight thirty Saturday evening by L. Vallone and five or six others:
>
> *"Questa proprieta e stata comperta dal commitato speciale por il populo Italiano di Cranston per donar la alla Nuova Chiesa Italiana."*
>
> The time for posting the above notice was well chosen. Next Saturday they celebrate their big feast Madonna della Civita. It would be a very bad time to interfere with them.
>
> My friend suggested to me that, since I am the pastor, I should go to you for permission to hold the annual procession of the statue, band, etc. Was he courting a refusal? Such a desire would be quite in accordance with his usual manner of acting. It would probably bolster up his plans.
>
> Father was on retreat last week when the notice was printed. However, he and some few Italian men stood in front of the billboard between the eight and nine o'clock Masses on Sunday morning, read and joked and laughed as well as pointed at the proclamation:

"Italiani diamo la nostra offerta cosi per 20 del prossimo Agosto possimo finirla dipagare. Non faciamo rideigli stranieri."

In the last issue of the *Cranston News* the enclosed clipping appeared. L. Vallone told the reporter for the *Journal* that they will take their case to Washington and if necessary to Rome. About thirty men assembled at Vallone's office two weeks ago.

Obediently yours,
T. H. Tiernan
July 16, 1923
(Diocese of Providence)

All the pleas and planning of the Italian population in Knightsville fell on deaf ears. The community and their leaders became angry. They felt the bishop was treating them unfairly.

The committee sent a series of letters demanding a response from the bishop. One of the last letters—dated May 22, 1923—that was sent to Bishop William A. Hickey was a strong message from the Italian community.

They wrote:

Most Reverend Sir:

The 8th day of May the Italian people of Cranston wrote you a letter in which they asked you to give them a permit to organize the new Italian Parish for which we have been waiting for over ten years but unfortunately we have had no answer either from you or the Italian priest.

The Italian people must have their own church at any price. On the 19th day of May the special committee united and voted to buy the land and notify you that if you don't give us a permit to organize a parish, they will build a church just the same, independent.

You have the Italian's peace and trouble in your own hands. The Italian people of Cranston choose peace providing they get their own parish and they are willing to pay for it.

They don't want the Protestants to laugh at them. They cannot sacrifice nearly 4,000 Italians without any church, priest or hall for 1,000 of St.

Ann's parishioners who have their own church priest, hall, and anything they ask for.

The Italian people ask you to give us a permit or to give us back the money you have in safekeeping for us. You must impress yourself that if the Italians don't get a permit they will stop going to St. Ann's Church just the same, so by delaying the permit you don't help anyone but only create trouble among the Italian people. We hope his time we will at least get an answer either affirmatively or negatively."

Your obedient Servants [156 legible signatures]
(Diocese of Providence)

Their message was finally heard after numerous letters from the Italian committee pleading for their own church. On April 12, 1925, the bishop created St. Mary's Church (Maria SS della Civita Parish, appointing Father Schettini as pastor and authorizing the new parish to use the former St. Ann's Church on Church Street).

Old St. Ann's Church-1858 (Cranston Historical Society)

Funeral of Dr. Alfonso B. Cardi age 30, held at
St. Ann's Church. Over 1000 people attended.

From the beginning, Father Schettini worked energetically to establish his parish on a solid foundation. By his action, he showed that he was more than equal to the responsibilities thrust upon him. He led his people spiritually by example. There was never one ounce of condescension in him. He felt that the people should work with, rather than for, him. He tried to immerse himself into their lives and become a part of them so he could better minister to their needs. His people regarded him as a father who adjudicated disputes and set the directions and tones for the newly formed parish family. No person was too small nor any problem too insignificant to command his attention.

Father Schettini directed that a fund-raising drive for a church be initiated almost immediately. The people were poor, but they still gave generously. The Depression had hit Rhode Island about six years before it devastated the rest of the country. In the midst of this time of economic upheaval, Father Schettini placed his trust in God and organized volunteers to canvas the Italian community to solicit contributions for their church.

Solicitors were sent out in pairs, and each donor was presented a passbook, in which his or her regular contribution was listed and acknowledged. Ninety percent of the money in the church fund came from the pennies, nickels, dimes, and quarters of the people who made the parish the recipient of their savings.

In addition to the fund-raising drive, Father Schettini did not ignore his other pastoral responsibilities. By 1935, the parish had grown to 671 families composed of more than 4,500 people. Sunday school was held in the church. A faculty of twenty-nine teachers directed classes to a total of 543 students. In addition, a number of parish societies also flourished. They were St. Ann's Society, Holy Name Society, St. Mary's Society, St. Aloysuis Guild, a chapter of the Third Order of St. Francis, a Children of Mary Society, and a St. Vincent de Paul Conference. This last group was especially important during the Depression. It aided many impoverished families of the parish through various works of mercy.

Father Schettini set an edifying example for his people by his own lifestyle. His living quarters consisted of an old farmhouse next to the church. He had it repaired and installed the necessities of living and moved in on April 15, 1925. By early 1935, there was sufficient money in the building fund to warrant the starting of a church (Diocese of Providence).

Two letters were written:

Reverend Father:

To purchase the property which the special committee is conveying to the Right Reverend Bishop for Italian Church purposes, the Committee accepted from the following named people the sums set opposite their respective names as loans to complete the purchase. It was understood and agreed that these loans were to be repaid to the lenders when the money became available to take up the notes given. The individuals forming the special Committee guaranteed to each lender the repayment of the money loaned and gave to each lender a demand note signed by each of the committee members, except for difference in names and amounts, in the following form:

$500.00 on demand after date we promise to pay to the order of Chiarina Manzo. Five hundred dollars at value received. August 15, 1923.
[signed]
Luigi Vallone
Frank P. Sinapi
Antonio Manzo
Nicola Biello
Antonio Cardi
Giuseppe Iannone

The following is a true, complete and accurate list of holders' outstanding notes:

Marietta Iannone	$100.00	31	Phenix Avenue Knightsville
Domenico D'Andrea	$500.00	1471	Park Avenue Knightsville
Maria Cardi	$100.00	1707	Cranston Street Knightsville
Chiarina Manzo	$500.00	1321	Cranston Street Knightsville
Ambrosio Sinapi	$500.00	204	Phenix Avenue Knightsville
Pietro Soscia	$600.00	556	Vermont Street Knightsville
Giuseppe Lorello	$500.00	22	Aldrich Avenue Knightsville
Antonio Saccoccia	$200.00	11	Knight Street Knightsville
Antonio Pezza	$300.00	1766	Cranston Street Knightsville
Michele Ialongo	$200.00	1707	Cranston Street Knightsville

January 4th, 1924
Luigi Vallone, Notary Public
Treasurer of the Special Committee
(Diocese of Providence)

The Aaron Haven Estate on Cranston Street was purchased by the committee for destination of the new Italian Church. On February 12, 1924, a letter was written to the bishop showing how the notes of the property were paid. Some donors had stipulations when they donated the funds. Others loaned money to the committee and were paid back in full.

> Domenico D'Andrea's note of $500.00. $350.00 was paid back, $150.00 was donated, and Antonio B. Cardi's note of $100.00 was surrendered with the condition their names would be placed in the entrance of the church. [This condition was never met.]

The letter continued,

> This note is a lawyer's hand so we are enclosing herewith checks to show payment. Upon the obtaining of this note it will be forwarded. The total of $2400.00 paid in full being the total amount of encumbrance on said property.

The Special Committee for the Italian Church kindly requests your Excellency for a receipt for those notes so that we may keep it for future reference.

Respectfully yours,
The Italian Committee for the new church,
Angelo Saccoccia
(Diocese of Providence)

Bishop William A. Hickey responded on February 9, 1925, in a letter to congratulate the Italian committee on the good work: "*You tell me you have succeeded in accomplishing with regard to the payment of notes on the house and land in Cranston.*"

He said, "*I expect to confer very soon with the Father in charge of the Catholics in the Knightsville section and I trust that everything will turn out satisfactorily.*"

Father Schettini found himself in a difficult position. He wanted to encourage his people, yet he had vowed obedience to his bishop. He asked his people to wait a little longer in the hope that Bishop Hickey would agree to their wishes. The young priest wrote to the bishop in a plea for some accommodation. He said, "*The Italian population of Cranston is full of good spirit, love, respect, and trust in their bishop and are ready to support and sacrifice for the erection of their own institution.*" The committee was willing to donate the land it had acquired to the bishop if he would establish the parish. Architectural drawings and plans for a church and hall were also submitted to the bishop's approval.

St. Ann's du oup,
Cranston, R.I.

Rt. Rev. Wm. A. Bialy, D.D.

Rt. Rev. Bishop:—

The following notice was posted on a large sign board (6 by 4) at 8.30 Saturday evening by L. Vallone and five or six others:
"Questa proprieta e stata comperta dal commitato speciali per il popolo Italiano di Cranston per donar la alla nuova Chiesa Italiana

Italiani diamo la nostra offerta cosi per 20 del prossimo Agosto possimo finirla di pagare. Non facciamo ridergli Stranieri. In the last issue of the Transion News the enclosed clipping appeared. L. Vallone told the reporter for the Journal that they will take their case to Washington & if necessary to Rome. About thirty men assembled at Vallone's office two weeks ago.

— Obediently yours
L. Hickman

July 16, 1923

The time for posting the above notice was well chosen. Next Saturday they celebrate their big feast — Madonna della Civita. It would be a very bad time to interfere with them. My friend suggested to me that, since I am the pastor, I should go to you for permission to hold the annual procession of the Statue, band etc. Was he courting a refusal? Such a desire would be quite in accordance with his usual manner of acting. It would probably bolster up his plans.

Then too Fr. was absent on retreat, last week when the notice was printed. However he + some few Italian men stood in front of the bill board, between the eight + nine o'clock Masses on Sunday morning, read, and joked and laughed as well as pointed at the proclamation.

F. H. Tiernan

Letter sent to Bishop W.A. Hickey by Fr. Tiernan (Diocese of Providence)

May 8, 1923

Right Reverend William A. Hickey
    Bishop of Providence R. I.

Most Reverend Sir,

It is over ten years that we Italians of the city of Cranston are working to have an Italian Parish and you most reverend gave us hope that our idea would soon be realized.

Your excellency knows the need of this new parish because there are over 500 Italian families in Cranston which amounts to over 3000 people. We feel the necessity of giving a religious education to our young ones and to organize ourselves within the customs and needs of the Italian people, which has been neglected for a long time. The actual state can not go on any further and is not usefull either the to American or Italian people because we can not progresse either spiritualy or economicaly. We refer not only to our idea but to the idea of the whole population and in order to escape trouble please provide us very soon and interest yourself with us as eaqualy as with other Italian colonies. In the name of the general committee we notify you that there are for sale 1½ lots of land and a big house for only $10,000. This is a splendid buy finan--cially and letting this go by would be a great economic loss to our people. Will you kindley come and look at this place as quickly as possible because there are others who wish to buy it.

Our representative Luigi Vallone promises you that the Italian people are ready to make any sacrifice with either money or work, and we repeat it again we will make any sacrifice providing you will deliver us from the present slavery and the continous persecutions of the American priest against all the Italians.

In regard to the present drive that you are promoting to build Catholic High Schools so our young ones can be educated in catholic ways, we Italians are ready to do our bit providing you give us permission to organize our own committee indipendent of Saint Ann's church

Your Obedient Servants

Luigi Vallone
Antonio Cardi
Antonio Manzo
Joseph Bottayuti

May. 22 1923

Right Reverened William A. Hickey
   Bishop of Providence R. I.

Most Reverened Sir,
     The 8th day of May the Italian people of Cranston wrote you a letter in which they asked you to give them a permit to organize the new Italian Parish for which we have been waiting for over ten years but unfortunatly we have had no answer either from you or the Italian priest.
  The Italian people of Cranston must have their own church at any price.
  The 19th day of May the special committee united and voted to buy the land and notify you that if you don't give us a permit to organize the parish they will build a church just the same , independant.
  You have the Italian's peace and trouble in your own hands. The Italian people of Cranston choose peace providing they get their own parish and they are willing to pay for it. They dont want the protastants to laugh at them . They cannot sacrifice nearly 4000 Italians without any church, preist or hall for 1000 of St. Ann's parisioners who have their own church preist, hall, and anything they ask for.
  The Italian people ask you to give us a permit or to give us back the money you have in safe keeping for us. You must impress yourself that if the Italians don't get a permit they will stop going to St. Ann's church just the same so by delaying the permit you dont help anyone but only create trouble among the Italian people.
  We hope that this time we will at least get an answer either affirmitively or negatively.

                                                   Your Obidient Servants

                                                Luigi Tallone
                                                Joseph DiBiase
                                                Nicola Briello
                                                Antonio Cardi
                                                Luigi DiSegna
                                                Antonio Manzo
                                                Giuseppe Sansone
                                                Francesco X Fusco

Giuseppe Maggiacomo 51 Knight St.
Antonio Soscia 37 Green st.
Pasquale Soscia 37 Green st
Salvattore ruggieri
Raffaele Pezzuco
Pasquale C. Sanoccia 13 Briggs St.,
Achille Scipione 12 Briggs st +
Squieri Francesco
Francesco Sapollo +
Luigi Di Legna 68 Colwell st cranston R.I.
Joseph De Ennis 68 Colwell St. R.I.
Antonio Ciano +
Vincenzo Ruggieri
August Ruggieri
Francesco Cerrito X
Francesco S. Selbonis
Alfonso Cerrito
Giuseppe Jannone
Paolo Ciono
Andrea Spirito
Domenico Spirito
Carlo Di Vona
Tomaso Meschino
1471 Park ave Domenico J. andrea

Nicola Biello
Tomaso Carnevale
Francesco Antonio Migliorelli
Enrico Rodi
Benedetto Sopranzo
Antonio Saccoccio 11 Knight Streett
Bambino Ruggiero
John Picaro
Vincenzo Caforio 1855 Cranston St
Antonio Del Bono
Antonio Giardino
Michel Caporicci
Nicolo Caporicci
Benedetto Saccoccia 1641 Cranston St.
Vincent Pezza   "   "
Ambrosio Giuliano +
Pasquale Paliotto
Vincenzo Mancini
Pasquale Manzi
Vincenzo Masella
Francesco Taranallo
Luigi Saccoccio.

	Serafino Fusco
Antonio Peggo	Tommaso Ciano
Thomas Riga	Domenico Langero
Charles Mancini	Francesco Notarianni
Gaetano Ruggieri	Francesco Fusco
Pompeo Corradini	Pasquale Soprano
Toni Pezzino	Giuseppe Livero
Gioacchino Notarianni	Erasmo Notarianni
Antonio Di Donato	Pasquale Magliocco
Frank Zacugo	Rocco Parrillo
Benedetto Saccoccio	Pasquale Paciofano
Del Bonis Pasquale	Pasquale Ruggieri
James V. Cardi	Giuseppe Palombo
Luigi Ruggieri	Francesco Paolo Pezza
Antonio Ruggieri	Francesco Mancini
Antonio Hawz	Antonio Simoce
Paolo Regu	Fedele Simonini
Antonio Parise	Cantivi
Giovanni Mangini	
Pasqual Larocca	
Salvatore Saccoccio	
Di not	

Pasqualino + Notariano
Gaetano Morrocco
De Simone Alessandro
Liberatore Ferrajano
Gaetano D'Alessio
A Tonio perrotto
di Lanzo Ferotero
cesere Dimeo
Michele Graziano
Tony Siudi
Paolotte Bambino
Antonio Saccoccio
Gaetano Izzi
Tom Fortunato
Stephen E Misto
Vito Parrillo   1599 Cranston St.
Loigi Di Jonzo +   1597 Cranston St
Antonio Morette
Gerardo Pagliarini   1583 Cranston Str.
Gerardo Zannella   1615 Cranston St.
Pasquale Squizzero   1627 Crans.
Giuseppe Lapella   1595 C.

Luigi Santurri 11 Knight St.
Domenico Pastore 1686 Cranston St.
Joseph Stravato 1677 Cranston St.
Salvatore Cruscione 1715 Cranston St.
Junior Merolla 1717 Cranston St.
Angelo Saccoccia 1723 Cranston Street
Nicholas Saccoccia 1721 Cranston St.
Antonio Sguizzero
Zannone Domenico
Luigi Ruggieri
Antonio Rossi
James Cerullo
Giovanni Gio
Domenico Cardi
Pasquale Palmaccio
Giovanni Ruggieri
Giovanni Cutola
Eraso paone +
Antonio Paccio
Michele Ruggieri
Frank Saccoccia
Giovanni Saccoccia
Pasquale Saccoccia 72 Gerani St.
Li Crudo
Vizio
Mirizzio X

Giuseppe D'aquila 1578 Cranston st
Francesco Moretti 1578
Antonio Rossi 21 Vicilance st
Luigi Spettuino 29 Rose St
Saverio Taicci 31 Rose St Cranston R.
Vincenzo Zonelli 27 Rose St Cranst
Frank Palumbo 14 Rose St. Cron
Green + Paliotto
Benedetto De Luco 35 Southern St., Cranst
Raffaele Manzo + 1337 Cranston St
Longino Quiccocio
Giovanni Antonio Coramute +
Angelo Crudele 41 New Hampshire sC

Letter and signed petition to Bishop W. A. Hickey (Diocese of Providence)

November 23, 1923.

Right Reverend William A. Hickey,
    Bishop of Providence, R. I.

    Compelled by continuos requests from the insistant Italian people and committee of Cranston, I think it is my duty to present to You the following situations.

    In expressing the ideas of the Italian people of Cranston I promise to be prompt and to obey faithfully what your most reverend would think is correct for the religious progress of this population. The special committee is ready to donate to you, as the head and administer of this diocese, the house and the land situated at Cranston Street opposite Haven Avenue, purchased with the intention to erect a new Italian church.

    This property was purchased and paid in full by the special committee. Actually the sum of $3250 has been paid from the funds collected by the committee with my cooperation, and $3000 has been loaned for the time being by the members of the committee with the intentions to have it returned, because they have already paid their own quota for the church. This has been the principal reason why the special committee never gave to you the warranty deeds for this property. If you would think it correct to pay this $3000 back with the money of the Italian people that you have in safe keeping, myself and the committee would promise you that we will pay it back within three or four months time.

    Enclosed you will find a sketch that Mr. Burrett D. Martin would draw for us free of charge; this shows the idea of the new hall and church for the Italian people of Cranston. It is for you, most reverend, to approve or modify this sketch so that we may start to do something. This church would be erected opposite Haven Avenue, on Cranston Street, so that the principal frontage would be seen from a quarter of a mile distant. The front wall will be of red brick construction, with casting stone trimming; the back and the sides in tile blocks; and the basement of cement. The proposed church will be 100' long and 50' wide, seating 600 persons. The ceiling will be flat so that it could easily be converted to a parochial school when progress and good future conditions of this parish will permit. This construction would cost approximately $25,000. I could never send you a specification with other details without your approval of this sketch.

It would be necessary to purchase four more lots of land next to this new property at the value of $4000, so the church would not be crowded and choked by private buildings, and it would be all right for the future progress of this parish.

The house which the committee bought is vacant, and would be a great loss without steam in the winter, so I ask you most reverend, to provide for it.

If you wish for me to express my view, I am sure that the Italian population of Cranston is, in general, full of good spirit, love, respect, and trust in their Bishop, and are ready to support other sacrifice for the erection of their own institution. At present the population is entirely quiet, but they never wanted to have anything to do with the St. Ann parish. They want their own independent parish; in other words they are waiting that you would provide for them at once.

Let me thank you in behalf of the Italian people and committee for the assurance that you gave to the members of the committee July 21. Only waiting anxiously for you to complete the work that has been started. Give us, most reverend, your practical decision. Whatever would be your decision, I am sure that it comes from an alighted and expert mind, from a paternal heart, because your love, most reverend, is the triumph of religion and humankind, so it is my duty to put in execution any of your orders.

Very happy to cooperate faithfully to this noble cause, and this worthy mission, I am,

Your humble servant,
Cesare Schettini

A letter Fr. Schettini wrote to Bishop W. A. Hickey,
Nov. 23, 1923 (Diocese of Providence

Y E. MIGLIORI, ENGINEER AND ARCHITECT, 524 WESTMINSTER STREET, PROVIDENCE, R. I.

SANTUARIO DI (SHRINE OF)
SANTA MARIA DELLA CIVITA
TO BE ERECTED IN CRANSTON, R. I.

GRANDE SOTTOSCRIZIONE
Per il
SANTUARIO
Di
S.ta Maria della Civita
Da essere Costruito in
CRANSTON, RHODE ISLAND
Secondo il
PROGETTO DI MASSIMA
Preparato dall'Ingegnere ERMINIO MIGLIORI
Approvato dal
Rt. Rev. William A. Hickey, D. D.
Vescovo di Providence

Graduatoria dei Sottoscrittori

DIPLOMA di 1.a Classe e Titolo di Fondatore per offerte da 100 dollari in su.

DIPLOMA di 2.a Classe e Titolo di Benefattore per offerte da 50 a 100 dollari.

DIPLOMA di 3.a Classe e Titolo di Contributore per offerte non minori di 25 dollari.

Donations of nickels, dimes, and quarters were recorded in passbooks (Larry Baldino)

;ignor _____

:o) _____

;ottoscritto per $ _____

NTARE SATO	DATA DEL VERSAMENTO	FIRMA DEL COLLETTORE

ALCUNI DATI IMPORTANTI

La chiesa sarà costruita in cemento armato, acciaio e mattoni. Il lavoro ornamentale esterno sarà in pietra artificiale, quello interno in "stucco" su armatura metallica.

Tre navate; altare maggiore e due altari laterali.

Due sacristie, ampio ed arioso sotterraneo.

Oltre 700 posti a sedere nelle navate.

Illuminazione elettrica e riscaldamento a vapore.

Costo circa $100,000.

Connazionali!

La grande sottoscrizione per l'erigendo Santuario in Cranston, R. I., viene aperta in nome di Dio, Ottimo, Massimo, e a gloria di Maria, nostra Augusta Patrona.

Il successo finanziario è nelle vostre mani, e dipende dalla vostra cooperazione e dal vostro sacrificio. Rispondete con entusiasmo all'appello, e date con amore, con generosità, oltre le vostre forze. Fate che il magnifico Tempio che oggi voi ammirate nel progetto di massima, sia al più presto, per il vostro concorso, una radiosa realtà.

Il Signore e l'Augusta Regina benediranno e ricompenseranno i vostri generosi sacrifici che vi siete imposti nel nome della Religione e della Patria.

Altri popoli si organizzano con tenacia, e progrediscono nel silenzio e nel lavoro.

ITALIANI! - Mostrate coi fatti di essere a nessuno inferiori e che, anche all'estero, continuate le nobili tradi-

recorded donations (Larry Baldino)

TO REV. FATHER SCHETTINI,

    ST. ANN'S,

        CRANSTON, R.I.

Reverend Father:

          To purchase the property which the Special Committee is conveying to the Right Reverend Bishop for Italian Church purposes, the Committee accepted from the following named people the sums set opposite their respective names as loans to complete the purchase. It was understood and agreed that these loans were to be repaid to the lenders when the money became available to take up the notes given. The individuals forming the Special Committee guaranteed to each lender the repayment of the money loaned and gave to each lender a demand note signed by each of the committee, except for difference in names and amounts, in the following form:

    "$500.   August 15th., 1923.

        On demand after date we promise to pay to the order of Chiarina Manzo Five Hundred Dollars at --- value received.

                (Signed)   Luigi Vallone
                              Frank P. Sinapi
                              Antonio Manzo
                              Nicola Biello
                              Antonio Cardi
                              Iannone Giuseppe "

The following is a true, complete and accurate list of holders of outstanding notes:

Marietta Iannone	$100	31 Phenix Avenue,	Knightsville
Domenico D'Andrea	$500	1471 Park Avenue,	Knightsville
Maria Cardi	$100	1707 Cranston Street,	Knightsville
Chiarina Manzo	$500	1821 Cranston Street,	Knightsville
Ambrosio Sinapi	$500	204 Phenix Avenue,	Knightsville
Pietro Soscia	$600	56 Vermont Street,	Knighsville
Giuseppe Lorello	$500	24 Aldrich Street,	Knightsville
Antonio Saccoccia	$200	11 Knight Street,	Knightsville
Antonio Pezza	$300	1766 Cranston Street,	Knightsville
Michele Ialongo	$200	1707 Cranston Street,	Knighsville

January 4th., 1924.

                                Luigi Vallone
                        As Treasurer of the Special Committee.

Subscribed and sworn to at Providence this 25th day of January A.D. 1924
                        John J. Sullivan
                            Notary Public

Record of donations and loans (Diocese of Providence)

Cranston, R.I., Feb. 12, 1924

Rtt. Rev. Bishop of Providence,

Providence, R.I.

The following is a statement showing how the notes of the property were paid.

Domenico D'Andrea Note for $500 accepted $350 and donated balance of $150 to church on condition that his name will be placed in the entrance of the new church.

Antonio Cardi Note for $100, surrenders his note free on condition that his name will appear in the entrance to the new church.

Antonio Saccoccia di Pasquale $200 Note Paid in full by Special Committee.

Michele Ialongo	Note for $200	"	"	"	"	"	"	"
Marietta Iannone	"	"	$100	"	"	"	"	"	"
Chiarina Manzo	"	"	$500	"	"	"	"		"
Antonio Pezza	"	"	$500	"	"	"	"	"	"
Ambrosio Sinapi	"	"	$500	"	"	"	"	"	"

This note is in a lawyer's hand so we are enclosing herewith checks to show payment. Upon the obtaining of this note it will be forwarded.

Total of $2400 Paid in Full being the total amount of encumbrance on said property.

The Special Committee for Italian Church kindly requests your Excellency for a receipt for these notes so that we may keep it for future reference.

Respectfully yours,

The Italian Committee for New Church

per *Angelo Saccoccia*

Record of note payments (Diocese of Providence)

copies of paid notes (Diocese of Providence)

$100.00   Aug. 15th.   1933

On demand   after date we promise to pay to the order of Maria Card
One hundred no/100   Dollars
at her home
Value received   Luigi Fallone
                        Frank N Singh
                        Antonio Manzo
No_____ Due_____   Nicola Diello
                        Antonio Cordi
                        Samone Giuseppe

Poster advertising fundraiser for the building of St. Mary's Church

Chapter 13
Societa Religiouse Pelligrinaggio Itrano

A certain group of impatient individuals from the Itrani community decided to take matters into their own hands. They did not want to wait any longer for a place of worship. A movement was started called the Societa Religiouse Pelligrinaggio Itrano.

Father Schettini wrote a letter to the Reverend Mother Provincial Teresa Saccucci:

> Reverend Mother Provincial,
>
> I feel it my duty to inform you that the father of young Maria Del Bonis is prepared to grant—free of charge—a piece of land that he owns, located on Vervena Street, for the building of an independent chapel, in opposition to our parish organization.
>
> I believe that he has been influenced by some irresponsible individuals, who would lead him to ruin. The local Curia has been informed and is surprised by the fact that Christian parents, who have a daughter who is a member of a religious congregation so respectable, would lend themselves to elements negative and harmful of our parish.
>
> Could you, Reverend Mother, with the tact and wisdom that distinguishes you, urge the good young Maria Del Bonis who is a member of your community, to wish to dissuade her own parents from making the wrong move, by giving their property for a purpose contrary to the religious interests of our colony.
>
> Your maternal intervention in cooperating in removing a cause that disturbs the religious organization of our parish, would be much appreciated, not only by me personally, but, I am sure, would earn the approval of the Superiors of Providence.

I would like you to remember me in your prayers, and accept my thanks in advance.

Most devotedly in Jesus Christ
Rev. Cesare Schettini
(Diocese of Providence)

A letter addressed to Bishop Francis Keough was mailed from the Villa Lucia, in Morristown, New Jersey, dated January 23, 1935:

Most Reverend and dear Bishop:

Having been informed of a certain matter which refers to a group of Italians of your diocese, I considered it my duty to ask the opinion of our Most Reverend Bishop and Superior Thomas J. Walsh concerning it. He in return, advised me to refer the matter to your Excellency.

Last June we received in our Community a young lady, Miss Mary Del Bonis of 36 Vervena Street, Cranston, Rhode Island. She was directed to come to this community by the Reverend Father Spiriti, O. M. of Our Lady of Pomei Parish, Baltimore, Maryland, who gave a mission last March in Saint Mary's Church, Cranston, Rhode Island, and was recommended for acceptance by the Reverend Father Schettini, her pastor.

On January 5, 1935, the Reverend Father Schettini informed me that an Italian Organization of Cranston was making preparations for the erection of an independent chapel. He further added you will note from the enclosed letters, that the local Curia in investigating the matter was surprised to find that the plot of land on which this independent chapel was to be erected was to be given by a person who has a daughter in religion, Mr. Del Bonis, the father of the young lady mentioned. Thus, Father Schettini asked me to have Miss Del Bonis try to persuade her father to not give the grant of land. I questioned the young lady on the matter and she said, that her father and members of the Organization to which he belonged have been contemplating the project for a long time, since they have not had the concession of having the Parish Church built. I had her write home to ask her father to please discontinue the project and in the meantime I also wrote to him. The reply to these letters was affirmative on the part of Mr. Del Bonis, but he referred this matter to the Organization, who, as you will see, from their letter, still persist in carrying on the project.

We are fully confident that your Excellency will take due measures in avoiding a schism among the Community of Italians as soon as possible. If you think, however, that our work, in which many of our Sisters are experienced in the apostolic field, will prove useful in bringing about a solution and aid in calming these souls, I shall willingly put them at your disposal for a few days.

Asking your Excellency to bless me and my Community, I am,
Devotedly yours in Xtc.
Mother Teresa Saccucci
Provincial of the Maestre Pie Filippini
(Diocese of Providence)

The Societa Religiouse Pelligrinaggio Itrano, on January 1935, responded to Mother Teresa:

Reverend Mother:

Consider this letter as if I am making a confession, explaining all the feelings of my heart and those of my companions. We had been the initiators to organize committees on behalf of construction of a church for the duration of 22 years. We have been the proponents of inviting the priest to be with us, so that through him, it would be possible that our desired dream come true.

Fourteen years have passed that the Italian colony endures with patience the continuous promises that follow from spring to autumn and autumn to spring without knowing anything positive. We find ourselves in the midst of a whirlwind of confusion without a light brightening the horizon, even though the people have shown and desire of the poor immigrants, already aged, (God, one at a time is calling them to Him), is not being respected; will die without the honor of seeing the new church.

The majority of these people come from the town of Itri, province of Rome, near Gaeta. There is in that small town a sanctuary where the image of Our Lady, Maria Santissima della Civita d'Itri, for which the people from Itri and other towns nearby have an unending faith.

The devotion of our great Mother vibrates in our hearts, also in these faraway lands. The feeling of nostalgia to see the protectress of Christians and of the people of Monte Civita honored soon is held with rejoicing of great love; the anxiety and expectation eat at our souls.

Seeing and considering that the promises have come to nothing, we have decided to build a chapel to be used simply to recite the Holy Rosary each evening and other common prayers; this is for the convenience of our neighborhood, especially for our women. This form of institution exists also in our native towns; because the Catholic Church is universal it means that private chapels as are permitted elsewhere should be permitted on these shores. These are not diabolic ideas, only thoughts sincere and pure. Yes, we are sinners, do not attend religious services; we are indifferent, reluctant, but under the ashes there is the fire, that is to say the everlasting flame of our religion that we have been taught in Italy and that is enough.

Reverend Mother, we are not children, our intelligence foresees that stratagem more or less hidden. We know who the author of this piece of news is, he does not want to lower himself to confer with us, perhaps because we are not worthy, but our Lord seeks to approach the unworthy ones and is comforted when he has converted the suspicious. Do not be astonished, Reverend Mother, even a person who worked as an assistant in the church of St. Ann, for greed to make money, expressed the wish, not directly from him, as many as 100 persons had guaranteed to pay $2.00 a month. We do not wish to make Mr. Del Bonis compromise; without him we will do the same if God wants, if he does not want, at his will. The honor of a reply from you would be welcome, perhaps it might bring forth something to soothe our anger.

Greatly devoted to your reverence, I bow with the greatest respect.

Religious Society of the Itrian Pilgrimage,
Antonio Manzo
(Diocese of Providence)

Despite the pleas to the Society of the Itrani Pilgrimage from church officials, an application for a permit to build the chapel from the city of Cranston was taken out on December 31, 1934. It stated the location of the chapel was Vervena Street, Plot 11, lot numbers 805 and 806. The owners were the Societa Pellegrinaggio Itrano.

The following was listed on the document:

Amount listed: $2500.00
Architect: Erminio Migliori
Builder: Michael Ialongo
Material: Cement Blocks
Number of buildings: One
Number of stories: Two
Entire height from sidewalk or ground: 31 feet
Building to be used for: Roman Catholic Chapel
Size of main building: 30 feet
Feet Front: 59' 4"
Land solid or filled: Solid
Footings rest on earth, rock, timber, concrete, or piles:
Thickness of foundation walls: 1' 4"
Material: Concrete
Outside covering of roof: Asphalt Shingles
How heated: Stove

The chapel at 41 C Street was sold to a private party and is presently a private home (Diocese of Providence).

APPLICATION FOR PERMIT TO BUILD.

BUILDING OF BRICK, STONE, &c.

Cranston, December 31 1934

To the Inspector of Buildings:

The undersigned hereby applies for permission to build, specified as follows:

1. **4th** Ward. $2,500.00
2. Street Location, **Vervena Street**
3. Plat, **#11** Lot No. **805 & 806**
4. Owner, **Societa Pellegrinaggio Itrano**
5. Architect, **Ermino Migliori, 31 Wealth Avenue, Providence, R. I.**
6. Builder, **Michael Iaolingo, 1698 Cranston Street, Cranston, R. I.**
7. Material, **Cement Blocks**
8. Number of Buildings, **One**
9. Number of stories each, **Two**
10. Entire height from sidewalk or ground, **31 ft.**
11. The building to be used for, **Roman Catholic Chapel**
12. State number of tenements, if for dwelling purposes.
13. Size of main building, **30'-0"** feet front. **59'-4"** feet deep.
14. Projections front, x Right side, x Left side, x Rear, x
15. Land, solid or filled, **Solid**
16. Footings rest on earth, rock, timber, concrete, or piles, **Earth**
17. Thickness of foundation walls, **1'-4"** Material used, **Concrete**
18. " " external "
19. " " party "
20. Are there any hollow walls? Thickness of same { Exterior { Interior
21. If girders are used to carry floors, state size, **(2) 29" I.B.**
22. Give distance between supports of girders, **16'-0"**
23. State longest distance between bearings of floor-joists, or beams, **9'-4"**
24. Give size of floor-joists, or beams, each floor **1st. 2"x9"   2nd 2"x8"**
25. Style of roof and material used, **Pitch   2"x8" Ralters**
26. Outside covering of roof, **Asphalt Shingles**
27. Any ventilator, elevator, or other inclosures above roof.
28. Material of cornice.
29. State what projections to be built over sidewalk.
30. No. of elevators For what use.
31. How heated (steam, water, or furnace), **Stove**
32. Any fire-places, if so, which stories?

Building permit for the Societa Pellegrinaggio
Itrano Chapel, 1934 (Diocese of Providence)

COPY

4 gennaio 1935

St.Mary's Rectory
1521 Cranston St.
Cranston,R.I.

Rev.Madre Provinciale,

    Sento il dovere d'informatla che il padre della giovane Maria Del Bonis, é disposto a cedere -gratis- un lotto di terra, di sua proprietá, sito a Vervena St. Cranston R.I., per la erezione di una Cappella indipendente, in opposizione alla nostra organizzazione parrocchiale.

    Credo ch'egli sia influenzato da alcuni individui irresponsabili, che lo guiderebbero alla rovina. La Curia locale é informata; e si é sorpresi del fatto che genitori cristiani, che hanno una figliuola che fa parte di una Congregazione Religiosa così rispettabile, si prestino al giuoco di elementi negativi e nocivi della nostra parrocchia.

    Potrebbe Ella,Reverenda Madre, con il tatto e la prudenza che la distinguono, esortare la brava giovane Maria Del Bonis, che fa parte della sua Comunitá, a voler dissuadere i proprii genitori dal fare un passo falso, col regalare la loro proprietá, per uno scopo contrario all'interesse religioso della nostra Colonia?

    Il suo materno intervento, nel cooperare a rimuovere una causa che perturba la organizzazione religiosa della nostra parrocchia, sarebbe molto apprezzato non solo da me personalmente, ma, son sicuro, riscuoterebbe ancora l'approvazione dei Superiori di Providence.

Voglia ricordarmi nelle sue preghiere, ed accogliere i miei ringraziamenti anticipati.

                                    Dev.mo in G.C.

                                    Rev.C.Schettini

Letter from Fr. Schettini to Mother Superior Teresa Saccucci, 1935 (Diocese of Providence)

COPY

Villa Lucia, 8 gennaio 1935

Pregiatissimo Sig.Del Bonis,

        Mi é pervenuta una notizia che mi ha sorpresa, ma non voglio e non posso crederla, poiché non é possibile che un uomo veramente cattolico come lei, possa prestarsi ad un fine veramente diabolico.

        Ho saputo che lei vuol donare un lotto di terra ad alcuni italiani per fabbricarvi una Cappella indipendente. Puó esser vero questo? Io voglio ritenere che questa notizia sia falsa e la prego a farmelo sapare subito.

        Donare il terreno per una Cappella indipendente vuol dire esser l'autore di tanti mali -di ribellione a Dio- viver fuori della Santa Chiesa Cattolica ed esser complice della ruina di infinitá di anime che si perderanno per tutta l'eternitá.

        Comprende Signor Del Bonis il grandissimo male che farebbe? Ma le ripeto non voglio pensarlo che lei abbia intenzione di far questo.

        Peró voglio metterla in guardia perché tante volte delle buone persone come lei, possono esser prese in inganno.

        Mi auguro di aver quanto prima una risposta che mi rassicuri di una cosa cosí importante, come la presente.

        Con i migliori saluti a lei e famiglia tutta. mi creda

Dev.ma in G.C.

Suor Teresa Saccucci

Letter sent to Luigi Del Bonis from Sr. Teresa Saccucci, 1935 (Diocese of Providence)

COPY

SOCIETÀ RELIGIOSE PELLEGRINAGGIO ITRANO
in
CRANSTON R.I.

Gennaio 14-1935

Reverenda Madre;
Nella presente, considera come mi stasse a fare una confessione, spiegando tutto il sentimento del mio cuore e quei dei miei compagni. Noi siamo stati gli iniziatori di organizzare comitati pro costruzione chiesa per la durata di circa 22 anni, siamo stati gli autori d'aver fatto venire il sacerdote presso di noi, affinché per mezzo suo si potesse avverare il sogno desiderato.
Sono passati 14 anni che la colonia italiana sopporta con pasienza le continue promesse che si succedono di primavera in autunno e autunno in primavera, senza che ancora di positivo si conosce. Ci troviamo in mezzo al turbine della confusione senza che una luce rischiarasse l'orizzonte, pure il popolo si é mostrato molto generose e fidente. Sono trascorsi molti anni e il desiderio dei poveri emigrandi giá invecchiati, il Signore a uno la volta se li chiama, senza che si ha l'onore di vedere la nuova chiesa.

La maggioranza di questo popolo proviene dal paese d'Itri provincia di Roma vicino Gaeta, esiste in quel paese un Santuario ove troneggia l'immagine di nostra Signora intitolata Maria SS. della Civita d'Itri, itrani e paesi vicini, hanno una fede infinita. La devozione della nostra grande Madre vibbra nei nostri petti anche in queste terre lontane. Il sentimento di nastalogia di vedere presto onorate la prodettrice dei cristiani e dei popoli dei monti Ciprei é attesa con giubile di grande amore, l'ansia e l'aspettativa ci rode l'anima. Visto e considerato che le promesse sono andate a monte, ci siamo decisi di fabbricare una cappella servibile semplicemente di recitare il santo Rosario seralmente e altre preghiere usuale, ciò é per la comoditá del nostro vicinato, specialmente per le nostre donne. Questa formola di istituzione, esiste anche nei nostri paesi nativi, giacché la chiesa cattolica é universale, significa che le cappelle private come sono permesse altrove, dovrebbe essere permesso in questi lidi. Niente ideie diaboliche, non pensieri singeri e puri, si, siamo peccatori, non frequentiamole pratiche religiose, siamo indifferenti, restii, ma sotto la cenera cé il fuoco, cioé la fiamma imperutiva della nostra religione, siamo stati educati in Italia é basta. Reverenda madre, non siamo ragazzi, la nostra indeligenza intravede i stratagemmi piú o meni siservati, sappiamo chi é l'autore di questa notizia.....non si vuole ribbassare di conferire con noi, certo non siamo degni, ma il nostro Signore, con chi non é degno, cerca d'avvicinarsi e si consola quando ha convertiti gli ombrosi. Non si meravigliasse reverenda madre, anche una persona che funzionava come assistente nella chiesa di S.Anna, per aviditá di far danaro, espresse la volontá altro che indipendente, basta che cento persone lo avessero garandito di pagare $2 al mese. Non vogliamo far compromettere il Signor Del Bonis, senza di lui faremo lostesso se Iddio vuole, se non vuole, a sua volontá. L'onore di una sua risposta, sarebbe gradita, forse potrebbe essere foriero di placare le nostre ire.

Devotissimo alla sua reverenza
m'inchino si sommo rispestto.

SOCIETÀ RELIGIOSE PELLEGRINAGGIO ITRANO
per.

Antonio Manzo

Letter sent to Sister Saccucci from Antonio Manzo, representing the Societa Religiose Pellegrinaggio Itrano 1935 (Diocese of Providence)

VILLA LUCIA
MORRISTOWN, N.J.

January 23, 1935

Most Rev. Francis P. Keough
Chancery Office
34 Fenner St.
Providence, R.I.

Most Reverend and dear Bishop:

        Having been informed of a certain matter which refers to a group of Italians of your diocese, I considered it my duty to ask the opinion of our Most Reverend Bishop and Superior Thomas J. Walsh concerning it. He in return, advised me to refer the matter to your Excellency.

        Last June we received in our Community a young lady, Miss Mary Del Bonis of 36 Vervena Street, Cranston, R.I. She was directed to come to this Community by the Reverend Father Spiriti, C.M., of our Lady Pompei parish, Baltimore, Maryland, who gave a Mission last March in Saint Mary's Church, Cranston, R.I; and recommended for acceptance by the Reverend Father Schettini, her Pastor.

        On January 5, 1935 the Reverend Father Schettini informed me that an Italian Organization of Cranston was making preparations for the erection of an independent chapel. He further adds, as you will note from the enclosed letters, that the local Curia in investigating the matter was surprised to find that the plot of land on which this independent chapel was to be erected was to be given by a person who has a daughter in religion, Mr. Del Bonis, the father of the young lady mentioned. Thus, Father Schettini asked me to have Miss Del Bonis try to persuade her father to not give the grant of land. I questioned the young lady on the matter and she said, that her father and members of the Organization to which he belonged have been contemplating the project for a long time, since they have not had the concession of having the Parish Church rebuilt. I had her write home to ask her father to please discontinue the project and in the meantime I also wrote to him. The reply to these letters was affirmative on the part of Mr. Del Bonis, but he referred this matter to the Organization, who, as you will see, from their letter, still persist in carrying on the project.

We are fully confident that your Excellency will take due measures in avoiding a schism among that Community of Italians as soon as possible. If you think, however, that our work, in which many of our Sisters are experienced in the apostolic field, will prove useful in bringing about a solution and aid in calming these souls, I shall willingly put them at your disposal for a few days.

Asking, your Excellency, to bless me and my Community, I am,

Devotedly yours in Xto.

Mother Teresa Saccucci

Provincial of the Maestre Pie Filippini

Letter sent to Bishop Keough from Mother Teresa Saccucci, 1935 (Diocese of Providence)

COPY

Cranston, R.I. 10-1-1935.

Egregia Provinciale,

       Subbito, mi preoccupa a scrivervi senza che si perde del tempo, siate tranquilli e non state in pensiere su di questo riguardo.

       Noi siamo Cristiani suguace di Dio, e seguiamo la nostra legge cattolica,

       Non é una chiesa che noi vogliamo fare é una cappella per nostra devozione, per metterci il quadro della Madonna della Civita perché noi siamo tanto devota di questa Vergine e una societá che noi abbiamo, non vi parla allungo, perché al piú presto ci vediamo, e ne parleremo a voce di questo affaro statevi tranquilli

       Con i cordiali saluti uniti a tutto il monastero mi dica vostra aff.mo

       Del Bonis Luigia

Letter sent to Sr. Teresa Saccucci from Luigi DelBonis, 1935 (Diocese of Providence)

APOSTOLIC DELEGATION

39/37

February 16, 1937.

Mr. Antonio Manzi,
86 C Street,
Cranston, R.I.

Dear Sir:

In the absence of His Excellency, the Apostolic Delegate, I acknowledge receipt of the letter of January 11th signed by yourself and Gabriele Susi.

Due inquiries have been made concerning the Chapel about which you write, and this Apostolic Delegation was surprised to learn that it was built not only without the permission of the Most Reverend Bishop of Providence, but even against his repeated warnings to the contrary.

It should not be necessary to remind Catholics that one of their very first duties is that of obedience to ecclesiastical authority. Your sad experience in connection with the building of the chapel in question should serve to impress this lesson upon all who took part in it.

I express the hope that henceforth all the good Italian people of Cranston will manifest a personal interest in their proper parish church, and cooperate wholeheartedly with the pastor who has been appointed to direct them in the way of salvation.

Wishing you every blessing, I remain,

Sincerely yours in Christ,

(Francis E. Hyland)
Secretary

Letter from Apostolic Delegation to Antonio Manzo, 1937
(Diocese of Providence)

APOSTOLIC DELEGATION
UNITED STATES OF AMERICA

1811 Biltmore Street
Washington, D.C.

N° 39/37
THIS NO SHOULD BE PREFIXED TO THE ANSWER

February 16, 1937.

The Most Rev. Francis P. Keough, D.D.,
Bishop of Providence,
30 Fenner Street,
Providence, R.I.

Your Excellency:

I beg leave to acknowledge with profound gratitude Your Excellency's esteemed favor of the 12th inst., addressed to Monsignor Vagnozzi, regarding the situation among the Italian people in Cranston.

I am enclosing herewith a copy of my reply to Mr. Manzi.

With sentiments of reverence and devotion, I beg to remain,

Your Excellency's
humble servant in Christ,

(Francis E. Hyland)
Secretary

Letter from Apostolic Delegation to Bishop
Keough, 1937 (Diocese of Providence)

Chapter 14
Plans for the Maria SS della Civita Church

Erminio Migliori, an architect, was sent to Itri to make architectural drawings of the church that housed the precious Madonna. The Italian immigrants wanted a church that most closely resembled the Itri shrine.

Plans called for an edifice of Italian Renaissance style of red brick with limestone trim. The diocese of Providence commissioned Ambrose J. Murphy, a famed architect, to design and organize the building of St. Mary's Church. Many local contractors submitted their names to work on the building of their new church. Ambrose Murphy chose the contractors that were approved by Bishop Francis P. Keough:

> General construction contract of Alfred Cianci, together with bond.
> Heating contract of Joseph P. Cuddigan, together with bond.
> Electrical contract of Brady Electrical Company, together with bond.
> A. Cardi Construction Co. excavation.

Groundbreaking ceremonies took place on Palm Sunday, April 14, 1935, the tenth anniversary of Father Schettini as pastor. Elaborate ceremonies were held at which all parish societies and other fraternal and civic organizations for the Italian people participated. More than 1,500 people attended and marched in the parade, which formed on the church property and in the vicinity of Haven Avenue and Church Street.

Procession from St. Rocco's Church to Knightsville.

It proceeded first through the Knightsville section and then to the Chestnut Grove section of the parish. Organizations that participated included the Holy Name and St. Vincent de Paul Societies, the League of the Sacred Heart, the Third Order of St. Francis, Our Lady della Civita Sodality, Our Lady della Valle Sodality, St. Ann's Society, the Sodality of Our Lady of the Assumption, and the Children of Mary.

Fr. Cesare Schettini

After the elaborate ceremonies and parade, Bishop Keough, Father Cesare Schettini, Judge Antonio Capotosto, and Maria Figliozzi Cardi (the widow of Antonio B. Cardi) turned the first piece of sod.

Maria Battista Figliozzii Cardi, 1935

A. Cardi Construction Co—Americo S. Cardi digging the foundation

Many other civic officials were present, including the Italian vice counsel of Providence. The memorable day concluded with benediction of the most Blessed Sacrament in old St. Ann's Church.

Construction of the magnificent church proceeded at a brisk pace. A wing of the rectory had to be removed to make way for the erection of the church soon after construction began (*Providence Visitor*). Within a year, the basement of the new church was completed, and first services were held there on April 5, 1936.

All shrines and furnishings were removed from old St. Ann's Church in a solemn observance following the completion of the parish's Lenten mission. Old St. Ann's, which had served the Italians since the parish's creation ten years earlier, was razed one month later as part of a plan to beautify the entrance to St. Ann's Cemetery.

Construction of St. Mary's Church occasioned a second round of donations by its parishioners. The large edifice was built of red brick and limestone trimmings in the Italian Renaissance style. The approach to the building is by means of a broad terrace with granite steps. There are three front entrances, all opening into a roomy vestibule. The principal facade has a stone and brick pediment supported on stone pilasters and featuring a rose window above the stone-framed center entrance.

On the gospel side, the front of the church is dominated by a sturdy campanile, at the base of which is one of the two secondary front entrances, the other being in a corresponding position on the Epistle side. The church proper has a lofty nave with a barrel-vaulted ceiling and is separated from the side aisles by arcades formed by column with ornamented capitals in the Italian Renaissance style.

The sanctuary is in a semicircular apse and has a high wainscoting of travertine stone surmounted by a series of niches for statues. The side-aisle walls are also wainscoted with travertine stone. On each side of the sanctuary, terminating the view down the side aisles, are the side-altar niches. Behind the latter, on opposite sides of the sanctuary, are the priests' sacristy and the altar boys' vestry, connected by an ambulatory, which passes behind the sanctuary. The sacristy and the vestry have separate entrances, which also give access to the church proper and to the basement. At the end opposite the sanctuary is the choir gallery, above the entrance vestibule. The confessionals are in niches in the exterior walls near the main entrance.

In the frontal of the altar are eight columns of green marble with capitals and bases of Carrara. The altar is flanked by kneeling angels of white Carrara, bearing electric candelabra. The church has a granolithic floor in tile pattern, and the roof is of red-clay tile. The basement is high and useful for social purposes when the upper church is completely furnished and if the basement chapel is no longer required (*Providence Visitor*).

The Carrara marble main altar, the statues of the Holy Angels, and the Last Supper were donated by Mr. and Mrs. Luigi Vallone, founder. The marble pulpit was given by Americo S. Cardi, in memory of his father Antonio B. Cardi founder. The two side altars, dedicated respectfully to Our Lady of the Valley and Santa Oliva, were donated by members and family from the town of Monticello Especia, Italy, and the people of St. Olive from Pontecorvo, Italy. The family of the late Luigi Merluzzo, one of the founders, placed the baptistery in the church. The holy water fonts came from James Moretti and Anthony Bona. The main and two side altars, along with the communion rail, and the bronze gates were carved at the studio of Angelo Lualdi in Florence, Italy. Many remaining necessities were donated by parishioners. The sacred pictures were painted by Angelone Metallo. According to one of the solicitors, it took two years to raise money for the altar railing and gates from more than one hundred families. He stated that he had to go back to a widow's home six times in order to collect twenty-five cents.

The lower chapel was used for the first time for Palm Mass on Sunday, April 5, 1936. As the congregation grew, the overflow of families went to mass in the lower chapel. Although Father Schettini planned that the lower chapel be used for the children's chapel and for social events, the lower chapel is still in use today for daily mass.

Unable to complete the erection of the main and side altars in time for early dedication and Easter services, masses in St. Mary's Church were sung March 28, 1937, at 7:00 a.m. and a high mass at 8:00 a.m. in the basement of the new edifice. The main altar was constructed in part on March 21, 1938, when the church received its first shipment of marble from Carrara. It was impossible and impractical for the services to be held upstairs in the main church due to lack of lighting fixtures and incompletion of the altar.

At long last, the new church, which was built for $100,000, was ready for its dedication. Bishop Keough came to the parish on July 3, 1938, to bless the cornerstone and officiate at the ceremonies.

Bishop Francis Keough at Dedication ceremonies

Blessing the corner stone of the church

The dreams of the Italian committee of seventeen years before had now become a reality. Father Schettini officiated at the first mass assisted by Reverend Peter Gorret and Reverend Louis D'Aleno.

Music for the ceremonies was provided by the St. Peter's (Warwick) parish choir and the new church organ. The remarkable instrument, which was built by Estey Company and installed by Lowe's Company of Beverly, Massachusetts, was fifty feet wide and contained 850 pipes. Professor Charles Doglio became the first choir director of St. Mary's Church until he retired, and his daughter, Mary, replaced him. The dedication ceremonies concluded the following week with a gala testimonial dinner honoring Father Schettini, following the emplacing of the Santa Maria SS della Civita statue over the exterior arc of the church's main entrance.

The Most Reverend Francis P. Keough presided at the dedication of the new St. Mary's Church on July 3, 1938.

Dedication of St. Mary's Church

    He praised the architect, the contractor, and the parishioners who contributed, through special gifts and funds, toward the new structure.
    The bishop warned the parishioners not to be content, now that they had given the church to God, but to continue their good work.
    He said, "*No matter how beautiful the gift you have given to Almighty God, no matter how much you embellish that gift, there is one gift that God wants, the gift of your own heart, the gift of your own soul. What he wants is to dominate, to dwell in, and to rule your souls and your hearts.*"

He asked the parishioners to be strict in their observance of the Ten Commandments and to attend mass and partake of the sacraments regularly.

"*God wants you to be strong and sturdy Christians. Catholics who will go forth and be strong to their faith. Catholics who know their faith and who, if necessary, will die for their faith.*"

During the dinner program, Father Schettini was presented with the receipted bill of sale for a new automobile bought by parishioners. The representation was made by Luigi Vallone. By the end of 1938, Father Schettini was ministering to more than 4,500 parishioners. It was clear that the size of his flocks had grown much larger than any one priest could handle. This was evident to Bishop Keough at the dedication ceremonies. On December 3, 1938, he assigned Reverend Oliver J. Bernasconi as assistant pastor.

Fr. Bernasconi, second pastor

Fr. Bernasconi and Giovanni Fabrizio in procession

On October 5, 1939, the construction of one of the most beautiful parochial residences in all of Rhode Island started. The two-hundred-year-old farmhouse was razed and replaced with the new rectory.

St. Mary's Rectory

The new St. Mary's Rectory was dedicated Sunday, June 23, 1940, with an impressive ceremony in the church. More than four hundred people attended. Supreme Court Judge Antonio Capotosto was among the invited guests. A dinner at one thirty opened the program with Councilman Walter Sepe as toastmaster (*Evening Bulletin* 1940).

A dinner was held on June 17, 1945, to honor Father Schettini and to burn the church mortgage. This accomplishment was no small feat. In less than ten years, the parish had amortized a debt of $125,000. When one considers the sad economic condition of the country during these years, the significance of the achievement becomes even more outstanding.

Father Schettini shared in the joys of the parish on that day, but he knew that there was still much more to be done. At the banquet, he set the tone for the parish's next few years by announcing that the major goal of St. Mary's would be a parish school. The tireless pastor knew that one of the best ways to solidify the parish's future was to build a school for the youth who would one day become the leaders of tomorrow (*Providence Journal*).

Waiting for the Madonna; Raphael Conte, Nicholas and Michael Giannini

Servant of God, Rev. Patrick Peyton with the Conte family, Ralph, Jr., Katherine, Bernadette and Ralph

Children who carried the rosary

Parish children carrying the 100 ft. rosary made of boating rope and red and blue roses. The rosary was made for the Diocesan Rosary Rally in 1970, in which the Servant of God Rev. Patrick Peyton was guest homilist.

children carrying the rosary during the procession.

Following the tradition of their ancestors, Zoe Conte and Kristiana Giannini prepare flowers for the arrival of the Madonna. The statue will be placed on a table in front of the Cardi Building on Cranston St. so that followers could honor her with flowers, and ask for graces and favors.

Katherine and Zoe Conte with Gaetanina and Kali Melone.

Krishan Melone at feast

Table prepared for the Madonna during the procession

Ralph and Zoe Conte

Michael Turelli faithfully carrying the cross of the 100 ft. rosary each year.

Edward Lanzi faithfully carrying the cross of the 100 ft. rosary

CHAPTER 15

A Pastor's Vision

The parish celebrated its silver jubilee in 1948, commemorating the struggles and accomplishments of Father Schettini and the Italian committee two and a half decades earlier. An honored guest at the festivities was the archbishop-designate of Baltimore, none other than Bishop Keough of Providence, who had supported and shared in so many of the parish's past achievements. Father Schettini, the priest who, for many years, walked the streets of Knightsville was instrumental in building the first and only all-Italian Roman Catholic church in Cranston and reiterated his wish for the initiation of plans for a school and convent at the jubilee ceremonies. Fate had other plans for the shepherd that was well loved by his flock (Diocese of Providence).

Many of us remember Father Schettini at his bedroom window, with a pillow supporting his head, peering out at the people after the celebration of the mass. We waited watching to see if his hand would rise in response, but he was much too weak. He watched while the statue was taken into the street for the procession to begin.

Children and elders in procession

The Italian Cultural Society waiting to enter the procession.

Elders of St. Mary's Church carrying the Madonna

The procession begins as the second statue of the Madonna leaves the church

The band playing solemn music headed the procession. Father Schettini's many friends and associates wept for their pastor and friend as they rallied around him with prayers and best wishes for a speedy recovery.

In 1947, Father Schettini became a citizen of the United States in a bedside court ceremony. The naturalization, unprecedented in Rhode Island, took place on July 1949. The candidate was presented by William M. Dalton, naturalization examiner, who told the courts under Judge John P. Hartigan that Father Schettini, a native from Italy, had all the qualifications of naturalization. When he was thought near death, and at the conclusion of the naturalization procedures of the United States District Court, at 10:00 a.m. in the rectory of St. Mary's Church, Neale D. Murphy, clerk of the court, administered the oath. Judge Hartigan was present. Father Schettini said in a weak voice, "*I am glad to be an American.*"

It had only been two years before the incident that Congress passed an act that would allow the sick and infirm who could not make the trip to the courtroom to become citizens by holding the district court outside the regular courtroom. (*Cranston City News*).

Still weak and frail, to everyone's surprise, Father Schettini recovered for a while and remained among his people, as a true shepherd and spiritual father.

Father Schettini never saw his dream become a reality. He died at 4:00 p.m. at St. Joseph's Hospital at the age of sixty-six on March 16, 1951. When Bishop Hickey first appointed Father Schettini as an assistant to St. Ann's in 1922, he never dreamed that the young Italian priest could rally his people and direct them to achieve the goals that the parish had attained. His thirty-year ministry was truly a legacy within the diocese. Father Schettini was much more than a "brick and mortar" priest. He led his people spiritually by example. His favorite view expressed to many parishioners was "*A parish without prayer is cold and sterile despite the beautiful buildings it may have.*" He was a man for his people and a man of God in every way (*Providence Visitor* 1947)

In September 1949, Father Bernasconi supervised the refurbishing of the church and the rectory. Two months later, Bishop McVinney made his first visit to the parish to officiate at the blessing of the church bells.

Church bells being blessed by Bishop Russell Mc Vinney

Church bells placed in bell tower (Providence Journal)

He announced the donation of the bells at the Madonna della Civita Festival in July 1949. The bells were blessed by Bishop McVinney at services on Friday night at the church. The bishop was assisted by Reverend Flaminio Parenti and Reverend John Drury as subdeacon.

Other priests taking part were the Reverend Charles Mahoney, the Reverend William Murray, the Reverend Patrick Canning, the Reverend Peter Gorret, the Reverend Attilio Bordignan, the Reverend Thomas Cassidy, the Reverend Nicholas Serror OP, the Reverend John Arnold OFM, the Reverend Roland Cardi, the Reverend John Tully, the Reverend Joseph Deignan, the Reverend Anthony De Angelis, the Reverend William Beane, the Reverend Joseph Lamb, the Reverend John McAlear, the Reverend Americo Lapati, the Reverend Alfred Santagata, the Reverend Angelo LaPolla, the Reverend Joseph Shanley, the Reverend Wilfred Gladu, and the Reverend Joseph Merluzzo. Father Schettini, who had been ill prior months, attended the services.

The first bell was donated by Mr. and Mrs. Joseph Ruggiere of Woodhaven, New York. The second bell was given by parishioners, and the third bell was given by Mr. and Mrs. Santi Campanella. The bells were completely electrified and could be sounded from both the rectory and sacristy. The bells were sounded at the Angelus three times a day (*Providence Journal*).

On June 2, 1950, a house at 19 Vallone Road was purchased for use as a convent for $9,500. A few months later, the last remaining debt from the construction mortgage of the rectory was paid off, enabling all their energies toward a realization of Father Schettini's dream.

Parishioners worked feverishly to renovate the convent building prior to the arrival of the sisters. The first floor of the two-story structure was converted into a nursery, with the second floor used as a sisters' residence. On January 31, 1951, Sister Superior Emma Del Corso and Sister Rose Iapaola arrived to establish the convent. They were members of the Institute of Maestre Pie Filippini. The order's aim was to instruct children in Christian doctrine.

Newly arrived Sisters

Reception for Sisters with local women (Anna Messori, Gaetanina Capotosto, Anna Mattera, and Marietta Iannone.

Slowly but surely, Father Bernasconi marshaled the energies of the parish behind the school project. Land was bought on December 1951 as a proposed site for the new school.

A few months later, additional land, both behind the school site and on which the former convent stands, was donated. A school-building fund was inaugurated in September of 1952. Simultaneous to the drive, the convent-school opened with a kindergarten of some twenty-eight students. Succeeding years saw the temporary school expanded by adding one grade each year until 1954.

The parish corporation voted to expend $300,000 for the construction of a new modern school in 1954. Actual work on the school began in March and proceeded at such a brisk pace that it was ready for the 1954-55 academic year, with Sister Superior Carmelo Lasco as principal. The school building was designed with the most modern facilities and conveniences available at the time. It contained eight classrooms, a visual-aid room, a library, and a gym. The Parents' Guild and parishioners supported their parish with the same energy that their forbears manifested to Father Schettini during the early 1920s. The aim of the school embodied this completely: "*to instill a Christian way of living based on a love of God and shown in the love of neighbor by willing involvement in those less fortunate than ourselves.*"

The convent was never meant to be permanent; it had outlived its usefulness. Ground was broken for the new convent on July 1, 1958. A year later, the convent was ready for occupancy. Funds were garnered to support the convent project through the annual parish reunion. Bishop McVinney was there to bless the convent and to lay the cornerstone of the school on June 14, 1959. A gala banquet was held that evening at Rhodes on the Pawtuxet to climax the ceremonies. Seven sisters moved into the convent following its dedication. The total worth of all parish properties was more than $1.1 million. It was a climax to thirty-six years of parish expansion, which had seen four new buildings erected since 1923.

In 1969, Father Bernasconi fulfilled his dream to build a parish center complex to alleviate the parish congestion. Father Bernasconi did not live to see the opening of the parish center. He died after a two-week illness on May 9, 1970.

Reverend Andrew Farina

Father Andrew P. Farina was appointed as Father Bernasconi's successor on September 8, 1970. He will always be remembered for his dedication to the parish youth, who have grown to be active adult parishioners with sons and daughters of their own, from the time he became pastor. He gave his all for the betterment of the parish. Father Farina supervised the completion of the parish center complex, which was dedicated by the late Bishop McVinney on June 13, 1971, only two years before his death.

Father Farina promoted the participation of the laity in the areas of administration, financing, education, the liturgy, and social action. In compliance with the directives of Vatican II and at the request of Bishop Gelineau, Father Farina implemented a parish planning and development committee for planning pastoral efforts and for managing the human and physical resources of St. Mary's Parish.

Keeping in step with the diocesan program of church renewal, Father Farina inaugurated a parish renovation program that had completely refurbished the church's exterior and interior to better meet the needs of today's modern church community. He cooperated with the parish's CYO program, and it continued to flourish and expand. St. Mary's CYO had built a reputation over the years of being one of the finest in the diocese.

I would not have researched the history of St. Mary's Church if it had not been for the request of Father Farina in 1975 and if I didn't have the full blessing of my late husband, Ralph. He always told me I was on the right road when things became difficult because of others' judgments. I didn't know it at the time, but it continued to be a tremendous grace for thirty-eight years for the opportunity and to be privileged to find so much information and documentation to share with you. I know Maria SS della Civita has led me every step of the way. I feel privileged to have had her in my home for thirty-six years and for God giving me a husband who always welcomed friends, family, strangers, clergy, and the religious into our home during a time of dire crises for those who needed prayers and healing for their loved ones.

Chapter 16

My Story

On July 21, 1975, St. Mary's Church was planning to celebrate their fiftieth anniversary. Reverend Andrew Farina, pastor of St. Mary's Church, inaugurated a parish renovation program to completely refurbish the interior and exterior of the church. Plans included the reconstruction of the main altar, moving it forward, making it the focal point of the sanctuary. One of the two sacristies was to be converted into a shrine room for personal devotions: the two side altars dedicated respectively to Madonna della Valle and Saint Oliva were moved into the new shrine room, and the tabernacle was moved from the center of the sanctuary to an altar on one side of the sanctuary. A new baptismal font was to be constructed and placed in front of the entrance to the shrine room. The plans also included the installation of new stained-glass windows throughout the church as well as new pews. The statuary in the church was also to be replaced by hand-carved wooden statues from Italy. Unfortunately, Father Farina did not get to witness the completion of the interior renovations of the church. He went to his eternal reward on January 10, 1976.

It was during the preparation for the fiftieth anniversary of the church that Father Farina telephoned me. He asked if I would come to the rectory to talk with him regarding researching and writing the history of St. Mary's Church. He stated that he was unsuccessful in obtaining information and pictures from parishioners after timelessly asking for help each Sunday. I agreed to meet with him.

Father Farina asked me what information or documents I had in my possession. He also asked me to help him achieve acquiring information about the parish history. I agreed to research the parish history on the condition that I didn't have to deal with a committee. At the time, I was deeply involved in a healing ministry within the Catholic Church and had little time for committee meetings. It took much sacrifice to work endless hours, months, and years to gather the information I share with you. I was blessed with a husband who knew the importance of this project and what it meant to me. He took care of family matters while I was out researching on microfilm and interviewing many of the elders in our community. With each bit of information I received, I tried to back it up with facts.

As I spoke and asked for their account of what happened in the Itrani community, I was impressed and deeply moved with the stories of our immigrant Itrani elders. The stories were always the same. They spoke with so much enthusiasm.

Their emotions were deep, and they spoke emphatically about the many hurts that were deep within them. My mother, Gaetanina Cardi Capotosto, brought up the subject of the original statue and urged me to go to St. Rocco's Church to inquire about it. When questioning the elders, they spoke of the statue with great emotion. The Italian people from Itri did not have their own church, so they would walk to St. Rocco's to prepare the statue for the novena, procession, and festivities.

I telephoned Reverend Joseph Scopa, pastor of St. Rocco's Church, and asked if I could speak with him. He agreed. When I arrived at his office, I told him I was researching the history of St. Mary's Church in Cranston and asked if he knew where the statue was. He wanted to verify I was not from any society before he would talk further with me. At my request, he telephoned Father Farina to verify what I had told him. Father Farina confirmed what I said, and he also told Father Scopa that he had given me complete authority to research the church history. Father Scopa, not knowing anything about the statue, asked the sacristan to talk with me.

The sacristan immediately told me the statue was stored downstairs in the basement, along with many other statues. I asked if I could see it and take a photo of it. He replied, "*Sure you can.*"

As he was unveiling the statue, covered with a white sheet, he said, "*I was going to give this statue to the Luigi Merluzzo family. Their father was a founder of St. Mary's Church.*" My heart was pounding with excitement as I gazed at this beautiful statue.

Bernadette Conte with the original statue

I asked, "*You were going to give it away? If that's the case, may I have it for our fiftieth anniversary?*" He continued to say, "*As long as the pastor approves you taking it, I don't have a problem with it.*"

We went upstairs again to speak to Father Scopa. Again he would agree and emphasized that as long as it was not for any society. I immediately went to St. Mary's rectory to speak to Father Farina. I was so ecstatic that the statue was coming home to her people. She had been stored in a church basement, covered with a sheet for many years. It was July 19, 1975, two days before our yearly official celebration, and the fiftieth anniversary of our church. I was in shock when Father Farina announced to me he did not have any use for the statue. He said, "*I ordered a beautiful wood-carved statue from Italy. What will I do with a plaster one?*" I tried to tell him the people would welcome her with open arms—that she would finally be home. He repeatedly said he didn't have any use for it. I could hardly believe what I was hearing. I asked him if I could take the statue.

He said, "*Yes, but what do you want with a plaster statue?*"

I told him I believed that Our Lady wanted to return to her people. They had gone through so much hardship, sacrificed much to provide us with a beautiful church and spiritual community—she belonged among them.

I could not let this opportunity pass. I never intended for the statue to stay with me or be mine alone. My intention was not to possess her or have control of her for myself, but I needed to be sure what to do with this precious statue. I had a deep sense she wanted to be in a place that all people could come to her in a time of crisis. I asked Michael Barnhart (the son-in-law of Virginia Soprano Piotti), who had a pickup truck, to go to St. Rocco's Church with my husband, Ralph, to get the statue. When they arrived at my home, they placed the statue on a large table in my backyard. Ralph and I viewed the damaged fingers, hands, and crown. Immediately, my husband and I began to restore the statue.

Matthew Izzo watching while his aunt Bernadette Conte restores the original statue.

I rebuilt the fingers and hands and repaired the crown. I saved chips of the original colors, and the statue was restored as it originally was. In the years she was under my care, the statue was restored three times.

Word got out quickly, and friends and neighbors came to view the statue, bringing a multitude of garden flowers.

Anna and Matthew Izzo placing flowers on the Madonna the morning of the feast at the Conte home.

Anna Migliori, Gaetanina Capotosto, Maria Civita Longo, Angelina Crudale, and Americo Cardi at Conte home.

I began to receive calls asking about the statue. Many asked what I was going to do with it. Others asked if they could come to my home to pray to her for a family miracle. Some claimed the statue belonged to them and would not listen to any explanation about what really transpired and how it fell into my hands.

I didn't have a clue that finding the statue and bringing it to my home would cause so much conflict over the thirty-six years she had been under my care. I never intended to keep her in my home, but every time I tried to plan building a shrine and museum for her so that future generations would have access to our history, I was met with much opposition and vindictiveness. I decided to let matters rest and to leave all in her hands. The spirituality I practice is true devotion to Jesus through Mary—*Totus Tuus*. If what I think she wants is really from her, then in her time it will come to pass.

St. Mary's had formed committees for the fiftieth-year celebration. Father Farina had gone to Italy. He had ordered the new statuary replacing the original statues, which were above the altar in separate naves. The second statue of the Madonna della Civita was in the center of the altar in a larger nave. The St. Mary's Feast Society would remove her the week of the feast and place her on the right side of the altar until the novena and feast was concluded. This statue was replaced with a wood-carved statue from Italy that was placed in the nave above the altar. The second statue remains in the candle or shrine room today and is brought out once again during our feast. She is decorated beautifully with flowers or with various types of canopies. In the earlier days, she was draped with gold jewelry that was given to her by devotees seeking a miracle or special favor.

Statue adorned with jewelry and money

During the absence of Father Farina, I received a call from one of the chairmen of the planning committee. She told me Father Peter Tedeschi and the committee did not want a book written of the history of St. Mary's Church. I told her that was fine with me. During my research, I had worked closely with the diocesan archivist for the fiftieth-year celebration, and we exchanged much information. She continued, "*But we would like to have your research information and documents.*" I responded by telling her I could not give the research to anyone. If they wanted someone else to write the history, the person selected needed to do the leg work in order to get the feeling of what the people really experienced. I felt it was laid to rest.

During a special meeting that was held concerning my involvement, some of the influential parishioners decided they did not want me to write the church history. At that meeting, a parish priest reasoned I had served on many diocesan committees and was an active lay minister in the Catholic Church. All fell on deaf ears.

The committee went around the issue in another way. They formed a historical committee and appointed one of my relatives to be the chairperson, and I was to be cochairperson. I told my relative I thought it was unfair to Father Farina, our pastor, to make these changes while he was away, and for this reason, I could not share the information with the committee, and I had made it very clear to the person who telephoned me without the approval of our pastor.

Although my husband, Ralph, is with the Lord, I am proud to say he never verbalized any objection to the multitude of people who called often to visit the statue and pray for a loved one who was sick or dying. People came from near and far, and often masses and prayer services were held at our home, with family, friends, clergy, and the religious. Whenever I was discouraged, Ralph would be the one to tell me not to give up and that I was on the right path. One of the last things he said to me before he passed on to the Lord was "*When you build the shrine, make sure there are tons of flowers around her.*"

We celebrated the feast day at our home for many years. The morning of the feast, my sister Anna Izzo's husband, Ronald, and Ralph would place the statue in the open hatch of our station wagon.

The original statue being driven through the streets of Cranston with Ralph Conte.

Ralph would sit with the statue, and Ronald would drive tooting the horn as they approached the neighboring streets. Neighbors and friends, many whose parents and ancestors were from Itri, would run outside at the sound of the horn, waving, holding vases of garden flowers, and singing their praises to the Madonna by echoing, "*Eviva Maria, Eviva Maria, Eviva Maria.*" When their journey was complete, the men placed the statue on a special podium in our backyard, and the neighbors would come with their beautiful garden flowers, honoring this beautiful image.

Katherine and Zoe Conte bringing flowers to the Madonna at Conte home the morning of the feast.

Yearly visitors from New York, New Jersey and Long Island. The Sinapi's, Di Biase's, and Fidelio families.

It didn't seem strange to me that when Ralph was in the hospital on the day we celebrated our feast in July 2000, from early morning 'til evening, many people—young and old—came to visit him, bringing flowers and religious medals. Priests and deacons also came to bless him. I said to him, "*Ralph, Our Lady is coming to you today. She knows the many years we celebrated her feast, and people brought flowers to her at our home.*"

He smiled. He passed away three days later on the feast of St. Ann, July 26, 2000.

CHAPTER 17
Home for the First Time

One day I was talking with Larry Baldino, who worked closely in our parish with our pastor at the time, Reverend James Verdelotti. The subject was about the feast. I said to him, "*Larry, when do you think the statue can come home?*"

He responded, "*We will pick her up on Saturday morning, if it's all right with you.*" Larry made plans with Ronald and Robert Bucci, and they came to my home with Ronald's pickup truck to take the original statue to St. Mary's Church.

Original statue leaving the Conte home

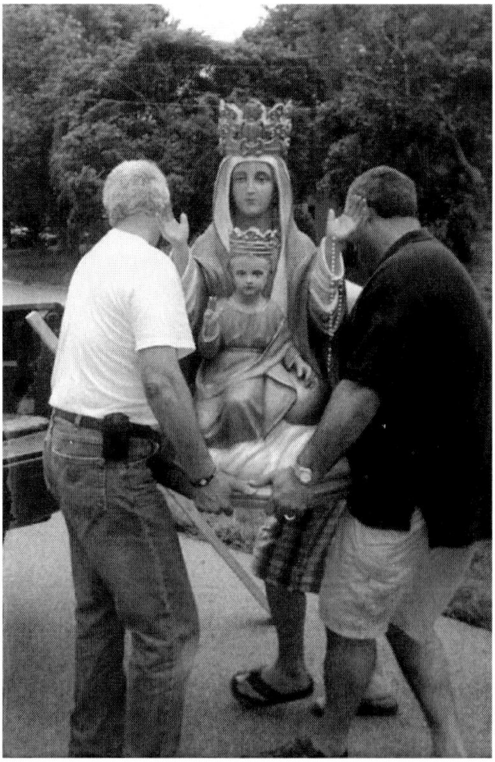

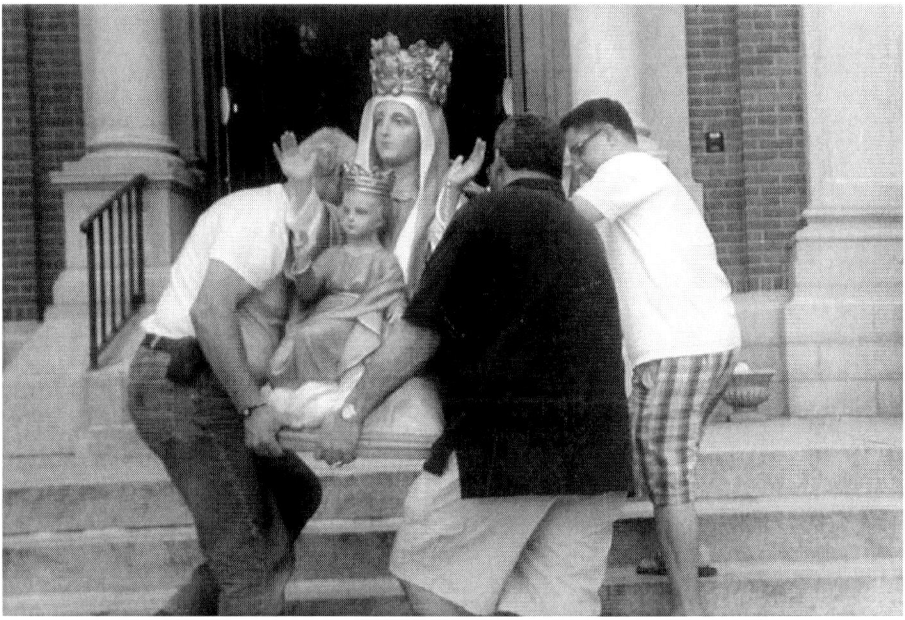

Original statue taken to St. Mary's Church for the first time by Ronald Bucci, Robert M. Bucci Jr., and Larry Baldino

It was an emotional and exciting day for me and for them. The men placed the statue in the candle room first and then in the nave on the left side of the altar. At all the masses, our pastor Reverend James Verdelotti explained to the parishioners that the statue was 105 years old and was on loan to them. The statue was to be returned to me until a permanent place of honor was designated for her and if the pastor decided he wanted her.

As the months passed and circumstances beyond anyone's control emerged, the cold winter days arrived. It was unsafe to move the statue in the frigid weather. The statue remained at the church.

Parishioners were elated that the Madonna was in the church. Many begged me not to take her back. I told them it was out of my hands. Although she remains in the church at this time, the decision whether to give her a permanent place at St. Mary's Church is not mine.

Until the day she left my home and was brought to St. Mary's Church, my home was open to anyone and everyone who wanted to pray before the statue of the Madonna in their time of crisis. I never solicited this practice; it started the day she entered my home. I knew this was what she wanted because she made it clear by the many people who called me to ask for prayers and intercession.

I am proud to share with the reader the information I have gathered during the years of my research. It has been laid to rest too long, and I now feel it is time to put on paper whatever information I have.

Although Fr. Cesare Schettini, along with Luigi Merluzzo and Antonio B. Cardi (my grandfather), and Luigi Vallone have been officially proclaimed founders of St. Mary's Church, my spirit tells me all our ancestors who came to a town called Knightsville are founders. Luigi Vallone, a man who led the community to see their vision come into reality, was a powerful spokesperson for the Italian committee. He became one of the first trustees, along with Antonio B. Cardi, of St. Mary's Church. They fought a good fight for themselves, their children, and future generations.

The account of which I write is based on facts. Everyone believes their fathers or grandfathers started the church and are the official founders. I can understand their feelings. When interviewing the elders, they spoke with such conviction of the persecution they suffered through many circumstances and the hands of people who knew so little about them and their culture. They were emotional about the hardships and sacrifices they made for the Italians to have their own church. How could one dispute their deep emotions and their belief that they were all the founders of St. Mary's Church? The documents I share with you will tell the story. I leave you to form your own opinion.

CHAPTER 18
Divine Intervention

My mother, Gaetanina, was legally blind at birth. When the child was a two, her mother, Maria Civita Saccoccio, died, leaving her six children. Gaetanina was the fifth child.

Maria Civita Saccoccio Cardi

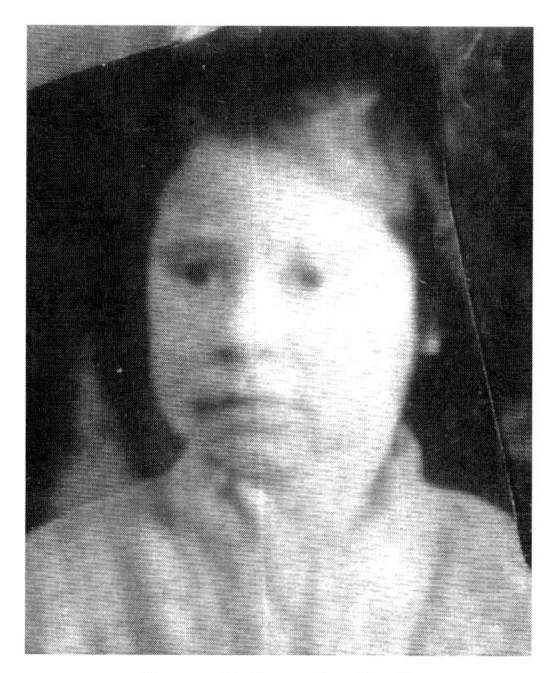

2 year old Gaetanina Cardi

Dr. Alfonso B. Cardi

Her elder brother, Alfonso, who later became a doctor, carried his sister on his shoulders and walked a long distance to the doctor's office each day for his sister to receive treatment. There didn't seem to be any solution for this child and her father, Antonio, was at a loss. When Gaetanina was four, in 1912, he decided to go to Italy with her to seek help and to marry Maria Battista Figliozzi, who became his second wife.

Grandparents Gaetana Pernarella and Alfonso Cardi

His parents, Gaetana and Alfonso Cardi, made arrangements for the child to be seen in a large hospital in Naples. Antonio's parents met their son and grandchild at the port of Naples. They had prearranged for the child to be seen by well-known specialists and immediately went to the hospital.

After a thorough examination and tests, the doctors told the parent and grandparents that nothing could be done for the child. They emphasized not to have anyone ever touch her eyes. Although everyone returned to Itri disappointed, the grandparents did not give up. Gaetana and Alfonso had a deep faith and lived a truly Christian life. They believed in the Madonna della Civita and her miracles. The grandparents were friendly with a woman who lived in Itri, who was known for her extraordinary gift of healing eyes.

Santina and Anna Maria Soprano (Dolly Haibon)

Anna Maria Soprano was contacted, and she agreed to treat the child. The entire town of Itri gathered together in support and prayer for Gaetanina and daily they gave many fresh eggs to Ann Maria to be used for her treatment.

After making a poultice with the beaten egg whites, Anna Maria placed the mixture over the child's eyes, and she then tied clean white linen over Gaetanina's eyes. This procedure was done several times daily for weeks, maybe even months. The community never stopped praying and giving their total support. When the proper time came, Anna Maria used prickly herbs, similar to sea herbs, to scrap the blood clots in the lids of the child's eyes and whatever parts of the eyes that needed scrapping.

When the treatment was complete, in the town square of Itri, while walking with her grandfather with the entire town watching, the blindfold was removed. Everyone waited in anticipation. The child began to cry with joy for she was able to see for the first time. Everyone present sang praises to the Madonna, and the gratitude they felt for Anna Maria lasted a lifetime.

Gaetanina remained in Itri and lived with her grandparents and her cousin, Reverend Roland Cardi.

Reverend Roland Cardi

Gaetanina Cardi and Cosmo Capotosto

After the death of her grandmother, she married my father at the age of twenty-one in Itri. Years later, Gaetanina was finally reunited with her family when she and my father came to America and settled in Knightsville. The story continues to be told years later by the few remaining people who are still alive to speak about it.

I have stated that, over the years, many individuals and families have requested to come to my home to pray in their time of crisis. I never dreamed I would personally go to the Madonna della Civita in my own desperation on June 17, 1978.

It was a warm and beautiful evening in which my entire family and friends were joining in the celebration of my mother's seventieth birthday with a party at her home. It was also the night of my high school class reunion.

My husband, Ralph, and I went to the class reunion when Mom's party was over. We mingled and enjoyed talking with my classmates and arrived home about 12:00 p.m. I had kicked off my high heels, and Ralph was in our bedroom to prepare for bed. My doorbell rang, and a policeman was standing there.

He asked, "*Mrs. Conte, may I come in?*"

I responded in panic, "*Of course. What has happened to my son?*"

He responded, "*Mrs. Conte, where is Mr. Conte?*" My husband came into our kitchen, and the officer said, "*We have been trying to reach you since 10:00 p.m. Here is a number to call in Florida. Your son was in an accident.*" He wished us luck and said he hoped all would turn out well.

I dialed the number, and Frank Gervasio's cousin, Mattie, answered. He said, "*Mrs. C, please put Mr. C on the phone.*"

I said, "*No, Mattie, tell me what is going on.*"

He repeated the request to talk with my husband. I handed Ralph the phone and heard him say, "*Okay, You're sure he is all right?*"

Ralph hung up the phone and said that Ralph had been in an accident, and he broke his arm. "*He is all right,*" he said. "*Go to bed now.*"

I said, "*Ralph would not have anyone call here to tell us he had broken his arm. He knows how worried I was when he and Frank Gervasio went to Florida on their motorcycles.*"

Ralph had completed one year of culinary school and wanted to search out work in Florida.

Ralph C. Conte Jr.

I had begged him not to go, especially on his motorcycle. I had a premonition that something was going to happen and saw him in a dream in a fetal position with a brace from head to toe. I wept for days begging the Lord to keep him safe.

One day while he was gone, I was driving to a store and was listening to the famous healer and preacher, Katherine Kulhman. She was preaching about Abraham and Isaac. She said the ultimate sacrifice is when Jesus asks us to give up a precious person, whom we love beyond everything, and to totally trust in him. It was as if a knife pierced my heart. I stopped the car and cried, "*But, Lord, he is my son. I love him. I can't give him up.*"

I don't know how long I was in my car weeping. After a long period of time, I finally said, "*Lord, I give Ralph and everything over to you.*" Two days later, Ralph telephoned me and said he and Frank arrived in Florida and were safe. He told me not to worry, that he was fine. Still I could not shake this feeling of dread.

I telephoned the number that was given to me by the police officer, and when Mattie answered, I said, "*Mattie, I forgot to ask what hospital Ralph is in.*" He gave me the name of the hospital, and when I hung up, I immediately called the information operator for the telephone number of the hospital. I told the person who answered that I was inquiring about my son.

She asked, "*Are you Mrs. Conte from Rhode Island?*" I said yes and asked about Ralph. She hesitated, then said, "*Mrs. Conte, will you be coming here?*"

"*What is wrong with Ralph?*" I asked. She said, "*Ralph was in a serious accident. He is in emergency surgery.*"

When I asked why he was in surgery, she continued, "*Your son is in shock, lost much blood, and has multiple injuries. The doctor who was on call and was formally from Rhode Island recognized the name and is trying to save his arm and his life. His arm has been practically severed, and his left arm is also injured. It is not good.*" I asked what other injuries he had, and she continued. I couldn't believe what I was hearing. She then said, "*Mrs. Conte, come as quickly as possible because your son may not be alive when you arrive.*"

I ran into the arms of the Blessed Mother, internally, and pleaded to the statue of the Madonna della Civita that was in my home. I begged her not to take my son, to save him. I felt as if I were giving him over to Jesus and then taking him back, begging for his life to be spared. My family came to my home, helping us to prepare to go to Florida as soon as the airlines called us with a flight. My sisters told me not to worry about my daughter, Katherine, who was sixteen years old at the time; she would stay with them.

Katherine boldly said, "*I'm going with you. Ralph is my brother, and I want to be there with him.*"

I looked at her and said, "*Yes, you need to be with us and your brother.*"

I asked my sisters, Anna Izzo and Marie Vartanian, to call Dr. Charles Simeone, a friend, and famous cancer researcher and surgeon, to ask him what top doctors he would suggest that I call when we arrived in Florida.

I will forever remember the sight I saw when I entered the hospital room. We wept when we saw our son, who was unconscious, with a multitude of tubes and machines keeping him alive. The blood was flowing into him, and it seemed it flowed out of him. His right arm was held up high in traction; he had bandages around his head, and his left arm was also bandaged and in another traction. He looked like the crucified Lord. It seemed there was so much equipment keeping Ralph alive.

I asked if a priest had come to anoint him. They said no but would call the local priest. A priest came and anointed him, and at my request, he came daily to bless Ralph and to give us courage.

I was told that a young man was driving and made an illegal left turn without warning as Ralph was driving on A1A in Fort Lauderdale, Florida. His bike went through the back door of the car, causing multiple critical injuries.

A young female jockey who lived in Florida was taking her neighbor to the same hospital Ralph would be taken to. As she was leaving the hospital, she saw the crowd and heard the conversations of the people who gathered around the scene of the accident. She ran over to Ralph as he lay on the ground, bleeding profusely. He was in severe shock. Linda Richmond held him and did not stop talking to him until he was brought to the hospital, which was on the same street. I will never forget Linda. I believe she was an angel sent by God to help Ralph stay alive. She came to the hospital daily to be with us and to wait to hear about his progress and was a great comfort to me and my family.

Each moment we faced a new crisis. After several weeks, Ralph and Katherine left for home, and I remained. It would be a long time for Ralph to remain in the hospital, fighting for his life. I telephoned the doctor that was highly recommended to me by Dr. Simeone when we arrived in Florida. He came immediately, looked over the situation, and came to the hospital each day to check on the progress and process of treatment and the condition of Ralph. Over the weeks and months, he guided me, advised me, and became a trusted friend to me.

I begged Jesus for direction and to give me guidance to make the right decisions. It seemed that each day brought a new series of crises.

One day, when I was facing another serious crisis and was feeling desperate, I received a phone call from a psychic I did not know. How he obtained my phone number was a mystery. As he introduced himself, he told me he had healed kings and queens and people from all over the world. He told me he had the stigmata and was featured in popular magazines and newspapers and was famous. I asked him, "*Do you believe that Jesus Christ is Lord?*"

He responded, "*Jesus was a man like me, a prophet, who preached and healed. I do the same thing. There is no difference between us.*"

I thanked him for calling me but told him I was not interested in his services and that I had all I needed in the Roman Catholic Church.

Weeping, I got on my knees, holding my Bible and rosary, and cried out to the Lord, "*Lord, I believe in all that you are, in your Holy Catholic Church, and in all that it holds. I believe in the sacraments, the anointing of the sick, and that you can still heal. I believe in miracles.*" I opened up my Bible and asked him to speak to me. My eyes fell on this passage from Sirach 38:1-9, Sickness and Death (*New American Bible*):

> Hold the physician in honor, for he is essential to you,
> and God it was who established his profession.
>
> From God the doctor has his wisdom,
> And the king provides for his sustenance.
>
> His knowledge makes the doctor distinguished,
> And gives him access to those in authority.

God makes the earth yield healing herbs
Which the prudent man should not neglect;

Was not the water sweetened by a twig
That men might learn his power?

He endows men with the knowledge
to glory in his mighty works,

Through which the doctor eases pain
And the druggist prepares his medicines;

Thus God's creative work continues without cease.
In its efficacy on the surface of the earth.

My son, when you are ill, delay not but pray to God
Who will heal you.

 I clung to this passage from beginning to end. It was a test in faith, especially when I was concerned with some of the decisions that were made by various physicians. I had contacted doctors and specialists throughout the world. My decision to stay with the doctors at Miriam Hospital, when we returned home, was because the team of Dr. Simeone were experts in this type of injury due to their experience with war injuries.

 One late afternoon, I was sitting by Ralph in the hospital room. His doctor came into the room. He came to the bed and touched the rosary I had hanging on the traction holding Ralph's arm upright. He smiled, and as he looked at me, he said, "*Keep it there. My grandfather had much faith in the rosary. It is powerful.*" He then asked me to step outside. He said, "*Ralph is in another crisis, and we are doing everything we can to save him. He has a blood clot now and other complications. He may not survive. You need to be prepared. Ralph watches your every expression, so please take a walk, get out your emotions, and come back into his room with a smile.*" I felt myself falling apart inside.

 I walked across the street to the beach. It was dark now as I walked along the shore. I was hysterical with grief and fear. I cried out to the Lord, "*Lord, help me. Help my son. I am here alone—I don't know what to do.*" As I looked into the water, I saw my shadow and a taller shadow behind mine. I then heard a voice say to me, "*But I said I will never abandon or forsake you. I will not leave you orphaned, even 'til the end of time.*" A peace that surpasses all understanding came over me, and I went back to the hospital. When the doctor came back in the room, he told me Ralph was better and had passed that crisis.

When Dr. A. began to doubt the experience of the medical team to further treat Ralph's complex injuries, he made arrangements for me to fly back home with Ralph when he felt it was safe enough for him to be moved and to fly. He made all the arrangements with Dr. Charles Simeone, at Miriam Hospital. We flew home, and Ralph was taken to Miriam Hospital where a team of doctors were prepared to treat him and to take over his case.

Dr. Simeone told me Ralph needed emergency surgery because when the doctors in Florida aligned the bones in his arm, they were not aligned at all, causing him excruciating pain, and the arm would never heal. Ralph went into emergency surgery for the correction of the bone alignment, with the grafting of bone and skin. I was not prepared for all the crises my family and I had to face. It seemed that over the five years that Ralph had multiple surgeries, lasting twelve to thirteen hours long, we faced many life-and-death crises and our faith was constantly tested. Ralph's right arm was totally paralyzed, and I was told it might have to be removed if it did not begin to regain motion. Pins were inserted in his arm, which protruded through his fingers. I forbade the doctors to amputate his arm, clinging to my faith and belief in miracles. If God brought him this far, he could also save him completely.

All through these years, I clung to Mary, our mother. People from all over the world prayed for Ralph, especially the people at St. Mary's Church, who gathered as a community in our parish church to pray for Ralph. Priests, lay leaders, and communities throughout the world prayed. Petitions and masses were held at holy shrines, such as Our Lady of Lourdes in France and the *santuario* of the Maria SS della Civita. Community leaders I knew from various states were contacted to pray for a miracle. Priests and lay leaders responded with much kindness. The complete miracle and healing was not spontaneous; it happened over a period of years through the skill of many doctors, just as the scripture said. The mere fact that Ralph lived beyond the first night of the accident is in itself a miracle.

After five years, Ralph came home permanently. I will always be grateful to Dr. Simeone, Dr. Carrol Silva, and others, especially the skilled neurosurgeon on the team who worked tirelessly to save Ralph's life and his arm. Ralph did not want any other doctors. He became close to this team and trusted them. Thankfully, Ralph did regain 85 percent use of his arm through many surgeries of muscle, nerve, and bone transplants and skin grafts.

After his full recuperation, Ralph went to live in Italy to study Italian cuisine and culture. He lived with relatives in Rome and Itri for a while, then moved to various regions, working and studying.

Ralph fulfilled his dream of becoming an award-winning chef and highly respected and acclaimed in the culinary industry. He became a proprietor of several successful restaurants. I have told him often that his greatest success is the fact that he became successful against all odds, especially when he was told by counselors, culinary instructors, and professionals that he would never be able to become a chef. He struggled with his handicap but rose above it and proved how wrong many well-intentioned people were.

I believe it was only through the graces of Our Lady that he could accomplish this. I also attribute it to the strength and determination of my daughter, Katherine, who brought her brother through many trying times and would not allow him to give in to death for one moment.

I know of many miracles or healing that can be attributed to Maria SS della Civita, especially the story of a young woman, Linda Scaralia Giordano, daughter of Ben and Hilda Scaralia.

Linda Scaralia Giordano

Ben was a trustee at St. Mary's Church in Cranston, and our families were lifelong friends.

Ben and Hilda had gone to Florida for the winter with Phyllis and Reginald Ricci, other lifelong friends of me and my family.

Annette Curelli, Gaetanina Capotosto, Phyllis Ricci, and Hilda Scaralia

Phyllis Ricci remembers the events as they happened. She and her husband, Reggie, were sharing an apartment with the Scaralias in Florida. The following is her account of what she remembered:

> "It was the winter of February 1996. Hilda and Ben Scarala went to Florida for a vacation in the sun. Shortly after arriving, Ben and Hilda received a telephone call from their daughter, Linda, informing them she had lung cancer and did not have much longer to live. Immediately, the couple left Florida to go home.
>
> They drove through the night and prayed continuously. As Hilda glanced out at the black sky, she told Ben she saw a vision. When she pointed it out to Ben, he also acknowledged it, saying it looked like an archangel.
>
> Upon their arrival at home, they prayed and were deeply worried. Bernadette organized a prayer service at St. Mary's Church, Cranston, Rhode Island, where many friends, relatives, and parishioners gathered to pray for Linda's recovery.
>
> Several weeks later, Bernadette Conte invited Ben and Hilda, along with her neighbors, Reggie and Phyllis, for dinner at her home. After a wonderful meal, the subject turned to Linda. Bernadette asked her guests if they would like to pray for Linda and write down their prayer intentions for the healing of Linda. They went into the prayer room, where Bernadette kept the statue of the Madonna della Civita. Hilda and Phyllis did so, and then Bernadette placed the intentions on the beautiful statue of the Blessed Mother that was in her home. She had previously discovered this historic icon in the basement of St. Rocco's Church in Johnston and, upon learning that it had stood idle for many years, had received permission to remove the precious statue from the church premises, putting it in a place of honor at home.
>
> Later on, Linda went to a scheduled appointment with her doctor. After his examination and review of her tests, he stated that, to his amazement, the tumor was completely gone, with only scar tissue remaining in its place!
>
> Family and friends rejoiced and gave prayerful thanks to the Blessed Mother of Mount Civita for this wonderful miracle.

Linda had not felt well for a long time. She suffered from a swollen and puffy face and sought the help of three different doctors without results as to why her face was swollen. She was told by one of them she had an allergy to cats.

When she went to another doctor, he took tests and chest x-rays, and she was admitted to and remained in the hospital. While in her room, Dr. Anthony Thomas, an oncologist, told her she had adenocarcinoma (inoperable lung cancer). When she asked how long she had to live, he told her three months with treatment. She immediately started three sessions of chemotherapy and forty sessions of radiation treatments. Everything looked so bleak for the Scaralias.

When Hilda and Ben arrived home, their family and friends rallied around them. The church was filled with people who came to pray for Linda. The scripture passage I used for the healing service that evening was from Matthew 9:20. A woman who was afflicted with hemorrhage for twelve years came up behind Jesus and touched the tassel of his cloak. The woman said to herself, "*If only I can touch his cloak, I shall be cured.*" Jesus turned around and saw her and said, "*Courage, daughter! Your faith has saved you.*" From that hour, the woman was cured.

Hilda wrote a request and placed it in a sealed envelope. The envelope remained in the prayer basket for years until the statue went on loan to St. Mary's Church on July 23, 1911. Linda still lives, and I write this story with her blessing.

Months later, Ben was diagnosed with the same kind of lung cancer Linda had. When Linda's doctor looked at Ben's x-rays, Linda was told he had mirror images with her x-rays. Both Ben and Hilda have passed away, Ben from lung cancer and Hilda from a car accident, shortly after Ben passed away.

I can recount a number of miracles, especially in my own family, but I chose to write about three medically impossible situations. Our ancestors lived and believed with all their hearts in miracles, and they passed this deep faith and belief to us. They gave their lives to Maria SS della Civita, who always brought them to Jesus, her son, and she in turn gave life back to them.

The lesson for us today is that God does perform miracles through the gifts (he gives to doctors, lay people, and priests), the anointing of the sick, the sacraments, and all that the church holds. He bestows his gifts on whomever he chooses for the greater glory of God. Healing is not always spontaneous. We need to be open to his Holy Spirit for guidance and accept the tremendous gifts he has given to individuals and our church and to realize the power of intercessory prayer. Jesus did promise us that if two or three are gathered in his name, there he will be. It is easy to forget when we are in a middle of an impossible crisis that nothing is impossible with God.

Chapter 19
My Trip to Italy

I flew to Rome, Italy, on April 17, 2013, with my nieces and one of their friends. We remained in Rome for several days. While my nieces toured Rome, I visited a dear friend, Rosealba Martini, and her husband, Georgio Belfiori.

Rosealba Martini and Georgio Belfiori

I could not have accomplished so much in a short time if it were not for Rosealba. Rosealba's mother, Agnes Martini, had a close relationship with Sister Teresa, principal of St. Mary's School. Agnes was a cook for the St. Mary's parish priests until Father Bernasoni passed away. Father Galliano Cavallaro was already transferred to Our Lady of Mount Carmel in Federal Hill. Rosealba recalls fondly the frequent visits Father Alfred Santagata made to their home on Valenti Drive. He missed the dinners Agnes cooked for the priests and loved going to the Martini home to savor the food.

I also remember fondly Father Santagata. He, as well as other priests from St. Mary's, loved to borrow my mother's spiritual books, especially books about Maria SS della Civita.

Rosealba attended St. Mary's School, went to the University of Rhode Island, and later returned to Italy with her parents. Her understanding of what I wanted to accomplish in Italy and her own experience with the St. Mary's community made my work easier.

She and I had several fabulous dinners with my cousin, Dr. Ettore Cardi, who also lives in Rome. Ettore had been chief of pediatrics and professor of medicine at the University of Rome, "La Sapienza."

Pope Giovanni Paolo 11, visiting La Sapienza Hospital, Pediatric Ward with Dr. Ettore Cardi, chief of Pediatrics (E. Cardi-Vatican Seal)

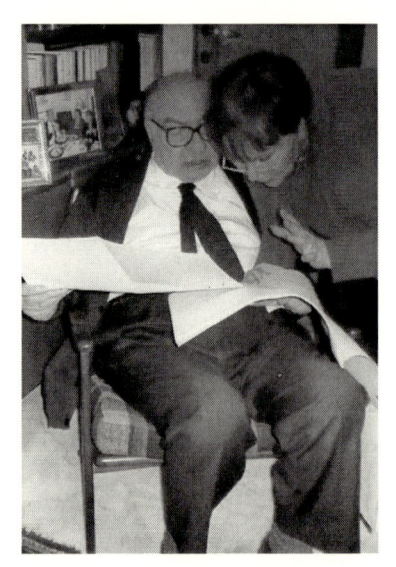

Dr. Ettore Cardi and Rosealba Martini Belfiori interpreting documents

Together, Roseabla and Ettore interpreted Italian literature for me. He knew I would be going to Itri for five days, and he called ahead to inform friends and relatives that I would be there on April 20-26, 2013. I spent much time in his home in Itri with relatives.

Being in Italy for a short time was difficult, especially when I had so much family history and further information on the Madonna della Civita to research. My cousin, Alfonso Di Biase, from Fondi, met me at the train station in Fondi, and after a wonderful dinner cooked and served by Fortunata, wife of his brother, Dr. Vincenzo Di Biase, Alfonso drove me to Itri.

Bernadette and Alfonso Di Biase in Itri

Cousins Dr. Vincenzo Di Biase, Alfonso Di Biase, and Patricia Perelli
Looking at old family pictures in Itri.

Zia Filomena Di Biase, with sons Alfonso and Vincenzo,
at the home of niece Patrizia Perelli and Paolo Ciarlantini

Dinner at Ettore Cardi's home in Itri with Lydia and Olinda Cardi,
Alfonso Di Biase, Ascanio Cardi, and Maria Rosaria Pesce.

He and other relatives spent much time with me looking through pictures and documents.

That evening I met with my cousin, Gianpaolo Cardi, and his wife, Paola Sepe.

Cousins Paola Sepe and Gianpaolo Cardi, Itri

Paola is the cousin of the noted author Pino Pecchia, whose reference I have made in many of the chapters. Paola is responsible for translating the Italian into English in the book *Tra Sacro e Profano in Terra d'Itri* she gave to me. They, along with others, guided and advised me how to accomplish whatever I needed to do.

I was greeted by Giovanni Ialongo, former mayor of Itri and one of the persons who was responsible (with John O'Leary, former mayor of Cranston, Rhode Island) in creating Knightsville and Itri as sister cities in 2002 (Gemellaggio). I had met the mayor and Mrs. Ialongo when they visited Raphael's restaurant in 2002.

Ralph Conte, Jr. Ralph and Dr. Frank Maggiacomo, and Mayor and Mrs. Giovanni Ialongo at Raphael's Restaurant.

John and Giovanni formed a nonprofit corporation called Gemellaggio. A resolution of the city council approved and affirmed the birth of the Gemellaggio.

Mayor and Mrs. Giovanni Ialongo with Mayor John O'Leary, 2000.

Mayor Giovanni Ialongo, Mayor John O'Leary at a reception at the Cranston Senior Center.

THE CITY OF CRANSTON

JOINT RESOLUTION OF THE CITY COUNCIL AND MAYOR O'LEARY

WELCOMING MAYOR GIOVANNI IALONGO AND HONORED GUESTS FROM ITRI, ITALY, AND AFFIRMING THE GEMELLAGGIO OF ITRI, ITALY, AND CRANSTON, RHODE ISLAND

*No.*2000-71

Passed: November 27, 2000

Kevin J. McAllister, Council President

Approved: November 27, 2000

John O'Leary, Mayor

WHEREAS, the sister-cities of Itri, Italy, and Cranston, Rhode Island, USA, enjoy a special relationship or Gemellaggio; and

WHEREAS, the bonds of friendship, as well as kinship, between the citizens of our sister-cities are deeply rooted; and

WHEREAS, our friends from Itri have journeyed far to visit us and strengthen the ties that bind our two communities.

NOW THEREFORE, BE IT RESOLVED, that Mayor John O'Leary and the members of the Cranston City Council wish to welcome our dear friends and open the doors of our City and the hearts of our people to Giovanni Ialongo, Mayor of the City of Itri, his niece Eleonora Golini, Antonio Gagliardi, Secretary of Itri, and his son Fabrizio Gagliardi, noted writer Alfredo Saccoccio, Christian Matrullo, Barbara Stamegna, Sarita LaRocca, Anna Lisa DelBove, Stefano Manzo, Daniele Agresti, Gemma Ciccone, Lucia Agresti, Maura Burali D'Arezzo, Laura Cariati, Vittoria Ialongo, Carla Stamegna, Igor Ruggieri, Roberta Pararlello, Patrizio Paparello who joins us from Los Angeles, California, Marco Soprano, Marina Riccardi, Silvia Fargiorgio, her husband Piero Dellavalle, and their two year old daughter Sara Dellavalle, Patrizia DeFalco, and Amalia Maggiacomo.

BE IT FURTHER RESOLVED, that our honored guests along with all the citizens of Itri, Italy, shall always be welcome in the City of Cranston.

The City of Cranston Resolution affirming the Gemellaggio
of Itri and Cranston (Cranston City Hall and John O'Leary)

-NOVEMBER 27, 2000-

554.

I. PUBLIC ACKNOWLEDGEMENTS AND COMMENDATIONS

INTRODUCTION BY MAYOR JOHN O'LEARY OF THE HONORABLE MAYOR GIOVANNI IALONGO, MAYOR OF ITRI, ITALY.

Mayor O'Leary introduced Mayor Ialongo, Mayor of Itri, Italy and welcomed him and his guests to the City. Mayor Ialongo addressed Mayor O'Leary, members of the City Council and members of the audience and thanked everyone for their warm welcome to the City.

RESOLUTION WELCOMING MAYOR GIOVANNI IALONGO AND GUESTS.

On motion by Councilman Aceto, seconded by Councilwoman McFarland, the above Resolution was adopted on a vote of 9-0. The following being recorded as voting "aye": Councilmen Mancini, Buttie, Councilwoman O'Hara, Councilman Hersey, Councilwoman McFarland, Councilmen Aceto, Carlino, DeLorenzo and Council President McAllister 9.

Mayor Ialongo presented the Mayor with gifts from Itri, Italy. Council President McAllister and Councilman Mancini presented Mayor Ialongo with a plaque from the members of the City Council.

Public Acknowledgment and Commendations, November 27, 2000
(John O'Leary)

The doors of the city and the hearts of the people were opened to Giovanni and those who traveled with him. Among the guests, along with students, that traveled with Giovanni and the group was noted writer and author Alfredo Saccoccio.

Being in Itri was exciting for me. I visited relatives and looked through volumes of family records and photos, always seeking new information about Itri and the *santuario*. I was amazed at some of the pictures I viewed once again. In 1975, Enrico Cardi and I looked through all the same books that he organized so well, as I again reviewed documentation and pictures during my trip of 2013 and eating the fabulous food cooked by Olinda Cardi.

Enrico Cardi and Bernadette Conte viewing historical
and family documents in Itri. (1975)

I visited the city hall, and Giovanni gave me a guided tour. He pointed out a framed painting on the wall of the mayor's office, painted by Maxwell May, illustrating the celebration of Madonna della Civita feast at St. Mary's Church in Cranston, Rhode Island, and a document when he and former Mayor O'Leary formed the Gemellaggio.

Maxwell May's painting of St. Mary's Feast and procession (John O'Leary)

He introduced me to many people at the city hall and walked with me along the streets of Itri as he pointed out many buildings of interest. During our walk, I met Giovanni Meschino and his mother Cesare, other relatives I hadn't known before. We sat at a local coffee shop with a well-known author, Mario La Rocca, as he and Giovanni autographed several important books about Itri, which they gave to me.

Giovanni Ialongo and Bernadette in mayor's office in Itri

Bernadette Conte with Giovanni Meschino, Itri

Amalia (Maggiacomo) and Pasquale Zanella preparing olives for me

Book signing in Itri, with Giovanni Ialongo and Mario La Rocco, author.

My cousins, Ascanio Cardi, and his mother, Olinda, took me to the Sanctuary of the Maria SS della Civita. It was a cold, rainy late afternoon, and we and a young woman were the only visitors. The three of us felt honored to have Father Francesco Vaccelli, a Passionist priest, offer the mass for our intentions.

Olinda and Ascanio Cardi with Fr. Francesco Vaccelli at the *santuario*.

After the mass, he led us to the back of the altar to explain and show us the icon of the Madonna. The antique painting was heavily grated. He pointed out the small piece of wood that was from the tree where the miracle first occurred, which was at the base of the painting.

Father Francesco then took us to the Miracle Room. He pointed out pictures and plaques, explaining the stories of people who received favors and miracles. The entire experience was touching.

Upon our departure, we glanced over the wall and could see Gaeta clearly. The rain had stopped now, and the view was clear and beautiful. It was peaceful, a peace one cannot describe—a peace that surpasses all understanding.

The church was magnificent. Above the altar was the painting of the Maria SS della Civita. As I turned around to see the choir loft, I was amazed of its beauty. Father Francesco played a CD of beautiful music that was familiar to me, especially because the elders in our community sang the same songs in church and during our processions in Knightsville. I felt so blessed. In my mind's eyes, I envisioned my parents and ancestors in this very church, along with all the elders from our parish and community. I could hear the echoes of their voices as they poured out their hearts in songs to *their* Blessed Mother. I felt a deep sense of loss and joy for knowing them. With my eyes closed and tears streaming down my face, I could see them reverently walking backward, facing the sanctuary in reverence to Our Lord and their precious Madonna, which was always placed on the right side of the altar, adorned with many flowers. Their intense gaze remained upon *their* Madonna as they continued to sing her praises, departing from the church at the conclusion of our novena.

Itrani women kneel before the statue of the Madonna,
lighting candles, and praying.

During my very first trip to Itri, in 1975, I visited the *santuario* with Reverend Lionel Blaine and a small group from Rhode Island Before celebrating the mass, the priest announced that my parents were from Itri, and he gave their names.

Bernadette, Fr. Lionel Blaine, and Enrico Cardi at the *santuario*, 1975.

Fr. Lionel Blaine offering mass at the *santuario*, 1975

The women, who wore colorful kerchiefs on their heads, turned to greet me and asked about my parents, whom they had known and remembered with fondness.

The native women during the Mass celebrated by Fr. Lionel Blaine, Itri, 1975.

It was an exciting moment in time for me to be in the homeland of my ancestors and to have a church filled with native women who remembered my parents and relatives.

After the mass, we were invited to have lunch with the Itrani people, who had come to the *santuario* in pilgrimage. They had an array of foods and drinks spread out on a picnic table and gladly offered to share their food and drinks with us.

Bernadette on the grounds of the *santuario* with pilgrims having a picnic, 1975

This practice is no longer allowed on the grounds of the sanctuary.

Inside the Church of Santa Maria Maggiore during mass.

Eviva Maria

I loved Santa Maria Maggiore Church (formerly the Annuziata), which I visited daily for mass and to simply go there to pray. I tried to envision the wedding ceremony of my parents, Gaetanina Cardi and Cosmo Capotosto, as I viewed the beauty and simplicity of the church. It was open all day, and in the evening, one could usually find some prayer group as they prayed and sang beautiful songs to the Lord. People of all ages gathered on the right side of the main altar. I felt a touch of heaven, listening and singing along with the parishioners.

Many came to pray before the silver statue of the Madonna della Civita and the beautiful plaster statue that is in a nave on the right side of the left altar. The magnificent silver statue is above the altar and is well protected from ill-intentioned people with a crystal glass pane and a grating.

The silver statue enclosed with a glass pane and grating

Statue of the Madonna della Civita in Santa Maria Maggiore Church, Itri

The large iron grating remains open during services and for visitors and parishioners so one can light a candle and pray and ask for graces from their Madonna. It was a beautiful sight to see, people praying before the Madonna della Civita. Some sit for hours in the pews in adoration.

CHAPTER 20

The Original Statue

To get back to the original statue I found in 1975 during my research, I was able to obtain a copy of the bill of sale for the statue from Rita Saccoccia Anderson, daughter of Nicola Saccoccia. When the statue was stored at St. Rocco's Church, because the Itrani community did not have a church, it became the property of St. Rocco's Church, and the Itrani people were unable to take possession of the statue they had purchased. I don't know why this happened or what the circumstances were for the pastor of St. Rocco's to have made this decision. It remained there until I found it.

Members of the community stated they had gone to St. Rocco's to gain control of the statue without success, and that the statue remained in the hands of a private party, despite many pleas from them to gain control. Whether or not anyone ever went to St. Rocco's to claim the statue is not certain. I cannot write someone else's history. I can only write what I know is the true story of my experience and what actually happened when I went to St. Rocco's Church and spoke to the pastor in 1975.

In all the years I lived in Cranston and attended St. Mary's Church, I had never heard of anyone mentioning the search for this statue. I did not have any ulterior motives when searching for her and remained focused on the research for the good of all the parishioners of St. Mary's Church and for all the Itrani community.

When I talked with the pastor and asked if I could have the statue for the people of St. Mary's Church, he made certain that I was not from any society before he released it to me. The statue remained in my care only because, unfortunately, Father Farina did not want it even though it was a major part of our history. It is my sincere belief that *the statue belongs in our upper church, in a place of honor*, for all our people. It does not belong to a selected few. Mary loves all her children equally. It seems clear to me, if Mary wanted anyone else to find her and to claim her, no power on earth would be able to stop it. I have tried over the years, without success, to talk with the priests at St. Mary's. An understandable situation is, when new pastors and parishioners come into a church without having the understanding of the faith, beliefs, and traditions, and without knowing the deep passion of the people for their past history, it is difficult for them to relate to such requests. Their views are often incorrect and complicated because of false information they have received from others.

As Father Farina said to me, "*It is only a plaster statue. What would I do with it?*" Our people know the statue is made of plaster. It was quite obvious he did not have an understanding of what this statue represented to the parishioners. For most of us, she represents the sacrifices of our ancestors who gave everything spiritually and materially to afford the opportunity to have their children and their offspring for all generations the freedom to practice their religion freely. They passed on their deep faith to each of us and will always be remembered with tremendous gratitude for giving us a beautiful church and a strong Christian community. That is what the statue represents to me and those who want to keep the legacy of our ancestors alive. She is a precious relic to us.

I cannot tell other people's stories and experiences; there will always be contradictions and conflicting stories. Her message to me was always the same and consistent: "*Let my people come. Let them ask. Let them pray. I will pour out my graces upon them.*" Isn't that what is really important? I believe we all want the same thing; only, we go about it differently. As the years have passed, and in meditating on the reason she allowed me to find her and to be her caretaker, my understanding is clearer: *I never claimed her as my own. She was the controller, the director of events, not me. I was simply clay in her hands.*

Everything happens for a reason and in God's time. One day I will finally know why I became the caretaker of the precious original statue of the Madonna della Civita and say thank you to Almighty God for entrusting her to me and my family.

Photo and Document Acknowledgments:

Rita Anderson
Larry Balldino
Mary Cardi Barone
Robert Bucci, Jr. (translator)
Antonio Cardi
Enrico Cardi
Dr. Ettore Cardi
Caterina "Gaetanina" Cardi Capotosto
Rev. Angelo Carusi
Bernadette M. Conte
Cranston City Hall
Cranston Historical Society
Cranston News
Arture Mari, D.D. De Meo, 2002
Diocese of Providence
Evening Bulletin
Maria Giannini (Back cover photo)
Linda Scaralia Giordano
Dolly Haibon
Marilyn Longo
Oaklawn Historical Society
John O'Leary
Don Virgilio Mancini
Sac. Ignazio Lombardini, 1976
Pat Maggiacomo
Sal Mancini
L. Marcella-Royal Crown Copyright (front cover)
Joanne Merluzzo
Antonio Pallotta
Arthur Pallotta
Barbara Palumbo
Pino Pecchia, 2003
Providence Journal
Providence News
Providence Visitor
A. Saccoccio, 1977

Made in United States
North Haven, CT
15 July 2023

38985260R00131